Conclusions of a Conservative

One Woman's Spiritual Journey

By
Nora Buttram

Cover by Terry Caturano

Shalom Publishing Co.

CONCLUSIONS OF A CONSERVATIVE
One Woman's Spiritual Journey

By
Nora Buttram

Shalom Publishing Co.

Author of earlier books:

GONE ARE THE DAYS
The Family Farm as it was and is

MORE THAN A JOB
Making a Difference one Mailbox at a Time

*Special thanks go to my daughter-in-law, Susan,
for help in editing.*

ISBN 978-0-9627057-2-4

51295 >

9 780962 705724

Printed in the United States of America
By
Gerald Printing Service
Bowling Green, KY

In Appreciation

to

My entire family

and

*All the people I have worshipped with through the years.
You have been a teacher, an inspirer,
an encourager, an adviser and much more.
Your friendship and fellowship has been
favored food for my fertile soul.*

Thank you.

*All proceeds from the sale of this book will
go to further the Kingdom of God on earth.*

Table of Contents

PREFACE

I realize that I am taking a bold step in writing on an issue of gigantic proportion and multiple opinions. An individual's religion is extremely important and very personal, as it should be. I would love to have a face to face conversation with each of you in order for you to share your spiritual experiences with me as this book does mine; since that isn't possible, I will get on with my end of the conversation.

I claim no credentials for being an expert or authority in any way. I do believe in the authority of the Bible and that is the basis for my understanding and commentary throughout this book. I also believe the Holy Spirit is necessary in helping us understand what we read. In John 14:17 Jesus said when the Holy Spirit came He would lead us into all truth, and in John 8:32 He says when we know the truth it will set us free.

In the 14th, 15th, 16th and 17th chapters of St. John Jesus explains to his disciples about the Holy Spirit and how He would come to take his place in their hearts after He returned to the Father. The first two chapters of Acts record that event and the miraculous things that followed. That same Holy Spirit is available to us today.

ONE NATION UNDER GOD

Thousands of years ago a guy named Amos predicted there would be a famine throughout the land—not a famine of food or a thirst for water, but a famine of hearing the words of the Lord.

Because of this same type of famine in our nation today many people may not have read the book of Amos in the Old Testament or know who he was. He was an ordinary person that God called to prophesy for Him. He was a farmer, a gatherer of sycamore fruit and a shepherd to whom God gave a special mission. He was to tell God's people that they had sinned and would be punished. The good part was that there was hope. If they would return to following God, He would make their nation great again.

In Psalms 33:10-19 (NIV) the writer says, *"The LORD foils the plans of the nations; he thwarts the purposes of the peoples. But the plans of the LORD stand firm forever, the purposes of his heart through all generations.*

Blessed is the nation whose God is the LORD, the people he chose for his inheritance. From heaven the LORD looks down and sees all mankind; from his dwelling place he watches all who live on earth--- he who forms the hearts of all, who considers everything they do. No king is saved by the size of his army; no warrior escapes by his great strength. A horse is a vain hope for deliverance; despite all its great strength it cannot save. But the eyes of the LORD are on those who fear him, on those who hope is in his unfailing love, to deliver them from death and keep them alive in famine."

I believe we have the same situation in America today as was in Amos' day and the same promise also. Like the Israelites, we have turned from seeking to follow God by reading and obeying His Word, to listening to what everyone else tells us. We seek our own pleasure and satisfaction rather than finding our joy and happiness in serving our Creator and seeking to please Him. I'm not surprised our nation is in trouble.

When I was a young girl we played the game 'gossip.' We sat in a circle. One person would start the game by deciding on a short sentence and whispering it quickly into the ear of the person on his or her right. This continued until it came back around the circle to the one that started it. The ending sentence was usually nothing like the beginning one.

Without intention, many truths are altered after leaving the original source. This is how Christians can be so far apart in their thinking. We listen to many different people, take the parts that we comprehend or choose to hear and like, and attach them to our belief system. Add to that the politically correct idea of 'everything is relative' and we come up with our own idea of what pleases God and convince ourselves that we are right. The truth is that it is what pleases us.

America today, also reminds me of the period of the judges in Israel. According to the earliest records this was an era of over 325 years from 1446 B.C. to 1105 B.C. During this time the book of Judges records the statement, *"Everyone did what was right in their own eyes,"* multiple times. Because of this philosophy the people lived in endless immorality and there was great violence in the land.

God would raise up men and women to lead the people in His way and it would work during their lifetime but when the leader died the people would return to their sinful ways. Maybe there is somewhat of an excuse for them, because during the times they had no leader to guide them by God's law, they were like lost sheep without a shepherd. Perhaps they had the laws God gave to Moses but most of the people were illiterate.

However, we are without excuse today. There is no reason to be illiterate, education is free and we have bibles everywhere. Even more important and available is the Holy Spirit to guide us. If there is a famine of hearing the Word of God in our land it is our own fault.

If there was no water in our land, every living thing would dry up and die. The same is true with our souls. Without the Word of God and the Holy Spirit, which is represented by water in the bible, our spirits will dry up and die. Surely that is what happens when we neglect to take advantage of the opportunity of seeking to know God and His will for us by reading and studying His Word.

I remember a story I heard about a very wealthy man who visited a coal mining camp in the mountains of Appalachia. He noticed that after walking miles to the camp to get to work, the miners had to walk up hundreds of steps into the coal mine to get to their job site. After returning home, the wealthy gentleman ordered an elevator installed to transport them up into the mine to their work.

Several months later he returned to see what progress had been made. How sad that he found only a few men using the elevator. Some did not trust it, some wanted to stick to their old way of doing things, many refused to use it because it was not their idea and others would not take the time or make the effort to find out how it worked.

God has provided a way for us to know Him through His Son, Jesus and the Holy Spirit. He has also preserved the directions for us in the Holy Scriptures. He paid all the cost and it is available to everyone. What shame that we do not take advantage of such an opportunity.

When our nation was founded in the eighteenth century our forefathers knew and relied on the scriptures to guide them. We see evidence of their dependence on it in every part of their lives from providing their daily bread to writing the constitution.

The old presidential memorials have multiple biblical quotes carved into them. The Rotunda of the United States Capitol displays religious artwork throughout. The Giant Bible of Mainz and the Gutenberg Bible are on prominent permanent display in the Library of Congress and bible verses are etched on the walls. In America's first Presidential Inauguration there were seven specific religious activities included. Some, but not all of them are still used today. Numerous quotes by past presidents can be found in preserved writings, such as:

Andrew Jackson, a Democrat, declared that the Bible **"is the rock on which our Republic rests."**

Abraham Lincoln, the first Republican president, declared that the Bible **"is the best gift God has given to men . . . But for it, we could not know right from wrong."**

Franklin D. Roosevelt, a Democrat, not only led the nation in a six-minute prayer during D-Day on June 6, 1944, but he also declared that, **"If we will not prepare to give all that we have and all that we are to preserve Christian civilization in our land, we shall go to destruction."**

Dwight D. Eisenhower, a Republican, declared that, **"Without God there could be no American form of government, nor an American way of life."**

In 1776, John Quincy Adams, who had been associated with many parties, said, **"It is religion and morality**

alone which can establish the principles upon which freedom can securely stand."

Not only was our government established on biblical truths and principles but our educational system as well.

Harvard University, the first institution of higher education established in the United States, and Yale University, the third, were founded by ministers. Princeton University, the fourth, was originally intended to train Presbyterian ministers. One of the main goals for these institutions and others was so that the bible could be taught and understood by the people.

In that same period most elementary and secondary schools used words from the bible to teach children their ABC's, how to read and write, grammar, literature, etc.

What happened? Why can the name of God not be mentioned in our schools today without interference by the ACLU saying it is against the constitution? The constitution has not changed. The Bible has not changed. Perhaps it is we, the people, who have changed. Perhaps we have gotten too busy or forgotten the importance of reading and understanding both documents. Perhaps it is time we recognized the famine we are in and do something about it.

Consider this excerpt from the Constitution.

"Amendment 1: Freedom of speech, religion, press, petition and assembly.

Congress shall make no law respecting an establishment of religion, or prohibiting the free exercise thereof; or abridging the freedom of speech, or of the press; or the right of the people a redress of grievances."

I understand that our public schools cannot emphasize one religion over another but neither can they keep anyone from exercising or speaking of their faith, be it Christian, Hindu, Muslin or whatever.

In view of this, why can the name of God not even be mentioned?   That is not freedom of religion, it is government mandated atheism.

It is not too late. In II Chronicles 7:14, God said, *"If my people, who are called by my Name will humble themselves and pray, seek my face and turn from their wicked ways, then I will hear from heaven, forgive their sins and heal their land."*

One of the best ways to seek God's face is to search his Word from beginning to end. Psalms 119 is the longest chapter in the Bible. Every one of the one hundred and seventy-six verses tells us how important God's words are as a guide to live by. Numerous other scriptures point out the riches of God's roadmap that he inspired men of old to write down for us.

Dare we be so lazy or ignorant to not take advantage of it?

WHAT CHURCH SHOULD I ATTEND?

My spirit was exalted, as I drove toward home on Sunday morning. I had attended worship services at two churches. They were very different, yet the same. One was where I attended with my family fifty to sixty years ago as I grew from a young child to adulthood; the other is where I attend now with my husband of almost fifty years.

The small country church of my childhood's congregation numbered around one hundred members and consisted largely of extended family members. All were hard working, lower income people with no more than a high school education and many times, not that much. Dress was conservative, living by the Bible was very important and commitment to church attendance and daily living of good morals were taught and encouraged. Baptisms were seldom and consisted mostly of family members coming of age. It was a General Baptist Church. My father led the congregational singing and my older sister and a cousin took turns playing the piano. After I got older, I played the piano part of the time. Our knowledge of music was very limited.

Today, this same church consists of a small increase in number of new people from the community and few of the original family members are left. They are still hard working, lower income people, with most having the equivalency of a high school education, more or less.

Little has changed about the teachings of the church but the dress code is more casual. There were two young people baptized today which is a more frequent occurrence than in former years. My cousin who played the piano years ago is still there and her husband leads the singing most of the time but they were in an accident recently and were not able to attend for a few weeks. I was asked to fill in for her and play the piano because they had no one else who could. The pastor's wife led the singing. She had a beautiful voice and was a good singer but had no formal training and a limited knowledge of music.

The other church I attended that morning recently ranked number sixteen in the number of baptisms from a list of all Southern Baptist Churches in the nation. In the last fifteen years it has grown from a small congregation of thirty people with a huge debt into a congregation of around five thousand. The church holds five services each Sunday and one on Wednesday evening. There are many activities going on during the week in the daytime and the evenings. We have built a very large multipurpose building and use it for the sanctuary plus other activities such as a gym. The old debt, plus the financing of the new building, was paid off in a short period. A new educational building is currently under construction for the many youth who attend. The dress is very casual, preaching is mostly evangelical. Bible study is encouraged and the praise worship and music is outstanding. There are numerous professional musicians and singers that contribute to the different services: enough to have four different worship teams that lead the Sunday services one week per month. People of many professions, bankers, financial consultants, film and computer engineers, dramatic artists, etc. use their expertise to contribute to and help manage the many activities of the church. People from all walks of life feel welcome. They range from very low income to affluent, white-collar worshippers. Many former addicts in the congregation have experienced true conversion in the last few years. I believe that I have seen more lives changed for the better here than at any church I know. That is one of the main reasons my husband and I choose to attend.

Today many talents were exhibited in a video and drama production that supported the pastor's sermon. There was also a baptism.

Driving home after the last service today, I contemplated the huge differences between the two churches and the worship services that I had attended. The culture was different, the abilities and the experiences of the worshipers' were extremely opposite, the presentations of the services were poles apart, yet the spirit was the same. Because of this, both congregations accomplished the same thing. The purpose of each church was to connect people with Jesus and tell them how the good news of the Gospel can change their lives, and then follow up by nurturing and encouraging them in their spiritual walk with God. The baptisms at both churches were truly meaningful. My heart was warmed and my spirit was lifted following each service and I could say with the Psalmist David, *"I was glad to have been in the House of the Lord."* (Psalms 122:1) I am amazed how God can use such different people, in different places, to create the Kingdom of God on earth. Actually, I should not be – knowing the limitless God that created us.

It disturbs me when I hear Christians speak negatively about another church that doesn't believe exactly as they do.

Recently I was eating at a truck stop and talking to a gentleman who was brought up in a Christian home and knew about the gospel. He is a big talker and I'm not sure if his questions were sincere or not but I am always glad to discuss spiritual things.

He asked the question, "What about the people in a certain church? Do they think one should not wear shorts or bathing suits?"

It seems he knew of someone who always wore long pants, even when on a boat, and would not get in the water. There could have been various reasons why this person did not want to wear shorts. She may have sincerely felt that in order to dress modestly, as the Bible says women should do in I Timothy 2: 9&10, that she should not wear shorts. Maybe she had a phobia about the water or she may have had scars she wanted to cover, but what my friend had heard was that it was because it was against the belief of her church. This may have been the case, and if so, there is nothing wrong with that. However, I'm sure there were many other things the members of this church practiced that were not as extreme and in agreement with the majority of Christian churches. Why was this one practice pointed out?

To further prove my point, another gentleman who was a very committed Christian commented, "The church down the street here will not allow women to take part in its leadership and another one I know of will not allow women to wear pants to the services or meetings there."

As far as I know, and the evidence was pretty convincing on both accounts, this information was true.

Again, my question is, "Why did he not mention that both of these churches believe that the most important thing in life is becoming a part of the Kingdom of God on earth?" Now, that would be something worth talking about!

Another common occurrence is what is known as 'church hopping.' Believers frequently move from one congregation to another. There are various reasons, some good, some, bad. Only God knows each heart and the needs of each person or family; sometimes those needs change and can be met better by another congregation. I would never tell someone where they should go to church. I would say that, if at all possible, when you leave one church to attend another it should be in the right spirit with good will toward all. Christians, more than anyone, should be able to get along with each other and disagree agreeably. If anyone has trouble believing this they should read the second chapter of I John.

Allow me to tell you a story about 'church hopping.'

A small ship was sailing unfamiliar waters and spotted a small island nearby. As they came closer the crew saw someone waving a white flag for help. When they got to the fellow who needed rescuing he told his story.

He said, "My small boat came apart many months ago and I have been living here by myself since then."

There were three shanty-like buildings that stood nearby.

The rescuer said, "What are those buildings for?"

The fellow pointed to one and said, "That is my house where I live and the one next to it is where I go to church."

The rescuer replied, "What is the other building for?"

"That is where I used to go to church," the fellow said.

THE NEW BIRTH

In America today, the popular consensus seems to be that there are millions of opinions about everything and no absolutes about anything. I believe this is because many people no longer believe that the Bible is truly the Word of God and can be trusted as a guideline for living their lives. As previously stated, I think that one of the reasons for this is the lack of knowing what the Bible says. It frustrates me that this applies to believers as well as nonbelievers. On the other hand, the Bible has been proven to be the way to abundant and successful living that gives purpose and meaning to our short stay on this earth.

It is no wonder that one verse says, *"Heaven and earth shall pass away but my words shall never pass away."* Mark 13:31 (NIV)

I think this means that no matter what comes or goes, God's words will never be changed or abolished. In view of this, it doesn't stand to reason that we spend most of our time learning about and accumulating things of this world that are only temporary while not even taking time or making an effort to seek eternal truths.

The scriptures warn us not to add to or take away anything from the words of this book or *"He will take away our hope of heaven."* (Duet. 4:1-4 & Rev. 22:18-19)

Christians believe the scriptures to be inspired by God. (II Timothy 3:16) Other scriptures give reference to this and also bear witness to the many prophesies that were given by men in the Old and New Testaments and fulfilled by Jesus during His life on earth. Even though the Bible has been translated many times from one language to another and in diverse ways, if God is God, He would have no problem keeping it without errors.

Through much study, prayer, contemplation and soul-searching I have the assurance in my own heart and mind that the Bible consists of absolute messages from God and can be trusted as a guideline for my life and/or anyone else's if it is followed. There is no better way that I can find that works as well.

Now that I have established why I trust in the Word of God, what is the first step?

In the young years of our life God instituted a plan for humans by giving us two parents of different genders in order to provide a balanced view of life for children both male and/or female. He instructed us, as parents, to care for and teach our children in the ways of the Lord until they come to the age of accountability where they can consider and work out the important issues of body and spirit for themselves. This might happen at different ages according to the degree of success the parents have performed their task. Physical needs of the body are easily apparent and do not usually have to be encouraged, children love making decisions on these matters. It is the spiritual needs that may need a bit more support, understanding and explaining. One reason is because we, as humans, have a tendency to want to do things our way instead of God's way. That was the problem in the beginning with Adam and Eve in the Garden of Eden and it hasn't changed. In fact, the decision Adam made in the garden is what caused us to be in such need of spiritual rescue. (Romans 5:12-21) I hope to help you understand more about this in a later chapter.

We are born with a sinful nature that will get us in more and more trouble as we grow older if that nature is not changed to a Godly one. This is what happens when we are 'born again'. Jesus explains this to Nicodemus in the third chapter of John, the third gospel; Paul explains it to us in Romans 10: verses 9 & 10 and it is emphasized throughout the whole of the Bible. This commandment is pretty hard to miss or ignore. It is, after all is said and done, the essential part of becoming a Christian. Paul tells us very plainly in the chapters preceding his admonition that no one is born into faith and is automatically a Christian because his parents and/or ancestors were. Some people use the term 'grandfathered in.' Paul also points out, in no uncertain terms, that we cannot attain our status as a Christian by 'good works.' We cannot earn our salvation no matter how 'good' we are or how many noble things we do for others. (Ephesians 2: 8&9) Jesus said in Luke 18:18 that no one is 'good' but the Father in heaven. He was telling about a rich young ruler who had come to him questioning about how he could be saved (have eternal life). The young man had either been misinformed or wanted to do things his own way. He had tried hard to keep all the laws but Jesus could see right into his heart and recognize his motives. Because of this, Jesus told him to go and sell everything he had and give to the poor, then come follow him. He said if he would do this he would have treasure in heaven. Jesus knew that the young ruler's many possessions were more important to him than anything else. Whatever is the most important thing in our life is our God. The commandments that he thought he had kept, clearly stated that God required his first allegiance, namely, *"Thou shall have no other Gods before me."* (Exodus 20: 3) Humans can be so sure they are right and still be wrong. Only God can reveal to us the extent of our unrighteousness and tell us what to do about it. That is the reason he instructed the rich young ruler to take such drastic actions. He may do the same with us.

To many people the big question is, and this is a very important question, "How does an individual obey this commandment? How is a person 'born again', 'saved,' 'converted,' 'regenerated,' 'confirmed,' or by whatever name one wants to call it?" Jesus said that we must be born again and Paul tells us how, but then, seemingly, Jesus confuses the issue by giving a special set of instructions to the rich young ruler.

It seems to me that Nicodemus, Jesus and Paul were speaking in general terms to everyone or anyone who was interested in becoming a Christian. On the other hand, when Jesus was instructing the young ruler he was speaking specifically to him. The spirit of a person is a very individual and personal thing. It belongs to them alone. No other person can control it, only another spirit, but we, the individual, can choose which spirit we allow in control. There are only two major spirits in our world, the Holy Spirit (a part of the Godhead) and Satan, who is an evil spirit and the Prince of this world. They are our choices.

The Bible teaches that we were born with Satan, the spirit of this world, in control because of Adam's sin in the Garden of Eden. (This is explained in Romans, chapter five.) In our natural born, human state, we are selfish and independent creatures who want to do things our way. You will notice this at an early age. Observe a two-year-old child and see what his or her actions convey.

Since we are born with this sinful nature in control, if we are to become a Christian and choose the other spirit (the Holy Spirit or God's way), we must willfully and purposefully make that choice. This is the point at which we are 'born again' in our spirit. Now God is in control instead of Satan. We choose His way instead of ours. Many times it takes drastic actions to get us to this point. Such was the situation in the case of the rich young ruler. He had always done things his way and did not want to give up being in control of his life. He turned away sorrowfully and did not choose eternal life. He was so attached to his way of life and his riches that he was not willing to give them up even if he could enjoy them for only a short time. He had a longing for something more than he was experiencing but did not have the faith that Jesus could or would provide it. This is where faith comes in. To be 'born again,' we must believe with all our heart that Jesus is who he said he was and know that by being one with God, we can trust him. The next step is confession with our mouth and water baptism. By being baptized we are signifying that the blood of Jesus has covered our sins, we have been forgiven, and are beginning a new life, clean and free. If true faith is there, we can't help but tell it! (Check out the third and fourth chapters of Acts and note especially Acts 4:20)

This regeneration is not uncomplicated in some ways. Over the years I have contemplated it quite a bit. At various times I have been moved to write my thoughts down in poetry form. I will share some of them with you on the following pages.

A Hunger Within

In the calm, dark stillness of morning,
While the stars and moon keep watch;
'Ore the soul that's deep in mourning
For the heart's sad, sorrowing plight.
Mid the silence in realms of the Spirit
My soul yearns to feel the presence
Of a God that knows each moment
Clothed in rapturous power and might.

Oh please ease my struggling hunger,
Feed it with the food of light;
Illuminating God in all His glory
On His throne so pure and white.
I will bow my head in honor
Lift my hands to receive the right;
A love that knows no bond or barrier
Power that overcomes mind and heart,
I now submit to my Lord and Savior
Who knew me from the very start.

I Stand Amazed

Great God of the Universe,
I stand amazed,
Knowing you know me,
Recognizing my utter dependence on you –
Even when I am unaware.
Protecting me in my weakness,
To show me how wrong I am;
When I think I am strong.

Loving me more than I can imagine,
When I deserve it the least--

Clearing the boulders,
Removing the obstructions
From my pathway,
Lighting the darkness
Created by my sin
That I longingly cling to.

Patiently, carefully, gently,
Lifting me from the pit,
Holding me in your arms
While I struggle and squirm
Trying to return again
To the familiar ways
That will eventually break my heart
And destroy my soul.

You know what is good for me,
You knew me from the womb,
So, you don't let me go
Until I have struggled free
Of the chains of destruction
That had bound me so tightly.

Now you release me,
Sit my feet on level ground,
You have taught me well;
How great is your grace and mercy--

My eyes are finally open,
My ears can hear your voice,
My body bends to my knees,
My hands lift up to you –
Thank you, Great God of the Universe,
For knowing and loving me--
I stand amazed!

God's Gift to Us

To know you know there is a God
To feel it deeply in heart and mind
To be set free by a faith so strong
It transcends all space and time.
It's hard to describe the way I feel
When God's Spirit enters my soul
And pierces my heart with His love
That redeems by his grace divine.

Weightless drifting through the air
Like floating clouds borne on wings;
Feeling the buoyancy of swelling tides
Lifting my spirit to realms of ecstasy;
Breathing deeply the fragrant scents,
Like blossoms swaying in the breeze;
Imagining their bouquets hovering,
Encasing each sweet breath of life-

My heart is full, my spirit is soaring
I've been revived by life's love song
Releasing the power of life's mystery
Revealing the soul's true worth.
Realizing anew the purpose to live
With meaning, far greater than self
Ready to face each challenging foe,
Courage to give it my very best

Let us go back to the rich young ruler. Money was not the problem, it was his unwillingness to let go of it. In I Timothy 6:10, Paul reminds us that not money, but, *"The love of money, is the root of all evil."* (KJV) To the rich young ruler, it was an addiction. An addiction is anything that is more important to us than allowing God to be our God. There are many of them in our modern world and

24

they are not just illicit sex, drugs and alcohol, although these are common and dangerous ones. Many addictions are honorable things when given their rightful place in our life, such as work, love for our children, parents, or anyone else. Politics is an addiction that has been seducing many intelligent people for years. Education is another. I believe 'political correctness' is leading the pack. Some of these can be very positive things in our lives and can enhance them greatly but none of them can take the place of God. He demands first place, not because he is arrogant or wants to be in control, but because he made us and knows the secrets to our assembly and smooth operation. This is all recorded throughout the Bible. It is difficult to point to specific verses and prove it and I suppose that is part of His plan too. He gave us all the scriptures and has preserved them through the ages, thus it must be important to study all of them. No matter where I read in the sixty-six books of the Bible, if I read enough to get the full concept of what it is saying, I am enlightened and inspired in my Christian walk. Many times, even one verse will stab my spirit. To me, 'stabbing my spirit' is making my spirit come alive, reminding me what a gift life is and renewing my zeal and enthusiasm for attacking the challenges of life with new faith and courage.

Since addictions are so varied and people so different, it stands to reason that God must use specific ways to bring about our salvation. Some of us are more attached to our addictions than others, yet all of us must give up our way and that is not an easy thing to do. The very young are more innocent and are very sincere when asking Jesus to 'come into their hearts'. God understands this and is pleased. He said in Luke 18:16, *Let the little children come unto me, and forbid them not: for of such is the kingdom of God.*" Once again, he can look into their hearts and know their motives. He knows if they are trusting in him. He even said in the next verse that we adults have to have this same kind of faith to enter the kingdom of heaven. The enlightened and intellectual age that we live in makes this even more difficult.

I am so glad that God does not see us as a herd of sheep or cattle. He sees each of us as an individual lamb and treats us as one. When we are seeking to know him and work out our salvation he deals with us in a personal way. That is the reason we can never tell another person exactly how they must be saved. God is the creator. You can tell from the world around us. He is not boring. He hardly ever does the same thing in the same way twice. In Mark 8:22-25 Jesus makes a blind man see by spitting on his eyes and putting his hands on them. A few verses later in Mark 10:46-52 (KJV) he healed blind Bartimaeus by only saying *"Go thy way; thy faith hath made thee whole."* (KJV) He accomplished the very same thing in two different ways. We don't know why. It should not matter to us. We know that God knows best how to bring each of us to him when we truly seek him. One of the many promises God makes in His word that He will not fail to keep is this, *"Ask, and it shall be given; seek, and ye shall find; knock, and it shall be opened unto you. For he that asketh, receiveth; he that seeketh, findeth, and he that knocks, it shall be opened unto him."* Matthew 7:7 (KJV) Notice, He does not say when this will happen.

I suppose I write of this because in the community where I have always lived there is much controversy among people who attend 'country churches' and 'city churches.' (This is how they are frequently addressed so for lack of a better title, I will do the same.) The people who attend 'country churches' do not trust that one can be saved in a 'city church.' This is because they believe one must go to a 'mourner's bench' at the front of the church and mourn for a certain amount of time. Sometimes it may take days, weeks or even years before the seeker receives salvation. It is according to the person's faith and if the Spirit passes by to do His work. This assumption is different according to the theory of the one who says it. Many have the idea that in 'city churches' a person is allowed, even encouraged, to just walk up to the front of the church, shake the preacher's hand and then be baptized. This is supposedly how they become a Christian.

On the other hand, many of the people who attend 'city churches' do not understand at all the idea of 'mourning' at the altar, shouting, praying loud or the showing of emotions that the people in the 'country churches' attribute to the Holy Spirit passing by, which is a must in the seeking of someone's salvation. Country church worshipers believe one must beg and plead for God to forgive their sins and save their souls. They do not understand the 'accepting the gift of salvation' or asking Jesus into our heart' as their city counterparts do and practice.

I will be the first to admit that I do not have all of the answers but I have contemplated these contrary beliefs quite a bit throughout my life. I am a 'seeker' and 'searcher' for the truth in any situation. I believe that 'spiritual things' are of the utmost importance in our lives. These different beliefs have brought about controversy and confusion in my family in different instances. Somehow, it doesn't seem right that 'spiritual things' should bring about confusion and discouragement in the lives of Christians. I do, of course, realize that Satan will use anything he possibly can to promote his cause and keep us from doing things God's way. We must remember that it is our choice which spirit we allow to control our mind and influence our beliefs and actions.

In my searching I have come to the conclusion that neither 'country' nor 'city' churches are right or wrong in principle or motive. Of course, God sees this much more clearly than I and makes the final judgment. When disagreeing with someone, if we are not careful we will lean too far in the opposite direction and be too extreme in our thinking. The church I grew up in was in the country but it probably had a more 'city' approach to being saved. From what I am able to surmise this may have been encouraged by some of the founders because of experience with what they termed as 'holy rollers' who were said to have literally gotten down in the floor and rolled around, contributing this action to the work of the Holy Ghost. (Holy Spirit) I say this with 'a grain of salt' because I wasn't there and I know how easy it is to exaggerate things we are not familiar with or dislike.

Our church believed in the Holy Spirit because it was a very biblical church but it was not something that was emphasized because it was not completely understood. Often, we are afraid of what we do not understand. It is also true that humans tend to stay with the familiar because there is safety and comfort there. This is sometimes referred to as our 'comfort zone' because we feel sure of ourselves within it and are uncomfortable if we venture from it in either a physical, mental, emotional or spiritual sense.

I believe it takes the power of the Holy Spirit to make Christians brave enough to venture into the unknown, especially in the spiritual realm. Since our church did not allow a large degree of that power into our midst because of lack of understanding, and fear, it was not available to teach us some of the things we needed to know. We struggled along, teaching our children the truths of the Bible as we understood them, encouraging good morals and commitment to the church. My parents were very dedicated to seeing that our family did not miss any of the church services. This was their way of giving God his rightful place in their lives. They taught us by word and by example that God should come first. Most of the time when parents are committed wholeheartedly to a religion, creed or philosophy it is very likely that their children will be too. This was true in my situation as well as my other five siblings. Our parents taught us the best they understood and I believe God was pleased with their offering. Many times throughout my life I have been reminded of how much I appreciate the fact that I was raised in a God-believing, church-going family. The good morals they taught us not only kept us physically healthy but kept us from many of the addictions that destroy people's lives and afflict them with pain and heartache.

However, I must quickly add that there is no guarantee that this will always be the case. God has his own agenda and I'm sure His plan is what will bring us complete fulfillment.

My exposure to church and serving God made me desire to know him better. The struggle has been a long one and, for sure, worth the effort. I am also convinced that the journey, and the learning that comes with the experiences, is what this earthly life is all about. One of my father's favorite scriptures that he quoted frequently was from James 4: 14. (NIV) It says, *"What is your life? You are a mist that appears for a little while and then vanishes."* He liked to paraphrase it by the quote, "This life is just a dressing room for eternity." Someday heaven and the new earth will be the reward, but I have often said that if there were no heaven I would still choose the peace and contentment of knowing our Creator on an intimate level in this life. It really is the best way to find happiness and fulfillment. Of course, according to the Bible, it is also the only way to get to heaven.

As a young child I heard older people tell about their 'experience' of being saved. Some had an 'out of body' experience; some saw lights and many said they would not take anything for the experience. Most everyone claimed that this experience was the assurance that God had saved them and they were on their way to heaven. As a child, I don't think going to heaven was as important to me as not going to hell.

Burning forever in a lake of fire that the preachers preached about with great passion was something I did not want to experience. They not only expounded on it from the pulpit but I could read it in the Bible and I had no doubt that it was true. (Different Christian denominations have different interpretations of this and I am not to say which is correct. Either one is bad enough for me! I personally believe what the Bible says about it.) Usually at a pretty young age, children are encouraged to be saved. My motivation, and probably that of many others, was by a large part the fear of hell; and in part by what we had been taught from the bible and hopefully by the wooing of the Holy Spirit. Perhaps all of it was ordained by God.

Today, there is much criticism about the old way of preaching about 'hell' and scaring people into being 'saved.' I do believe there is a lot of merit in promoting God's love and longing for all of us to be his children, and this cannot be emphasized enough. Probably the most quoted verse in all the bible is John 3:16. (KJV) It says *"For God so loved the world that He gave His only begotten son that whosoever believeth in Him should not perish but have everlasting life."* The next verse is very important as well but quoted less frequently. It says, *"For God sent not his son into the world to condemn the world but that the world through Him might be saved."* The book of Proverbs says in more than one place that *"The fear of the Lord is the beginning of wisdom."* I believe that wisdom will help us see the need to recognize, early on, the omnipotence, omniscience, omnipresence and awesomeness of God who has the power to do whatever he wishes or deems necessary for His plan to be carried out. I am so glad He is in control, not me!

From a very early age, I was exposed to people going to the altar and being saved. There were usually many tears and much rejoicing, plus testimonials from many of the people. Seemingly, when the spirit was present among the people, they were more free to express themselves to one another. I noticed that people who were usually prone to silence and few words, mostly men, would sometimes cry and tell people they loved them when they could not seem to otherwise. This 'spirit' definitely had an effect on people and most of the time it was shown in some form of emotions. John 3:8 compares the Holy Spirit to the wind. He said you can hear the sound of it, and you can see the effects of it (my words), but you cannot tell where it comes from or where it is going. It moves wherever it pleases. Because of this, one can understand why it would or could be a little hard to completely grasp by someone, especially young children.

Some of my thoughts about it came out in the form of poetry.

By the Spirit

"The flow of the stream,
 The flight of the bees,
 The meaning of the dream,
The breeze thru the trees;
 How can I change them or make them cease?
 There is no way and keep the peace.
 His way is infinite,
 There is none better,
 We just can't see it,
 It's not by the letter."

MY PERSONAL EXPERIENCE

One day at school some of the children were playing church at recess. It was a small country school with three classrooms and eight grades. I was about seven years old and probably in the second grade. Some of the older kids that attended church where I did were doing the preaching, singing, etc. When the part came to invite people to the altar, I went up. I was crying, perhaps because I am a very emotional person at times when my feelings are stirred and I'm sure the older kids thought it was really the spirit working in my heart. They prayed with me and asked if God had saved me. Being so young and probably wanting to please them, I said, 'Yes." I do remember the incident even today. I remember where we were at school and what kind of clothes I was wearing.

I was encouraged to tell my parents when I got home. Situations like this puts parents in a difficult position because they do not want to tell their child they are not saved because they cannot know for sure. About all they can do is be happy for them and that is what mine did. I later told the church that I was saved, joined as a member and was baptized with three or four other young people. For me, that was not the end of it, it was just the beginning. I did not think I really was saved because I did not have that 'experience' that I had heard others talk about. I felt guilty because I thought I was living a lie, and I kept struggling about how to know if I was saved or not. I prayed and prayed to God to help me and show me but he did not seem to hear my prayers. One day I was in inner turmoil and I walked away from the house to a wooded area where I could be alone, got on my knees and prayed for God to save me or let me know if he already had. I did not get an answer but when I came out of the woods, I looked up and in the sky I saw cloud formations that looked exactly like a common picture of that day with Jesus kneeling in prayer. I felt somewhat better and continued on as best I could, trying to serve God and have faith that I was his child.

Several years later after I had married and we had our family, I still was not satisfied that I was saved for certain. One day during worship service I went to the altar. I told the church how I felt and ask them to pray with me that I could know without a doubt about my salvation. I remember an uncle that I had quite a bit of confidence in telling me that I needed to just believe that I was saved. He did not tell me that the Bible says, *"For it is by grace you have been saved, through faith—and this not from yourselves, it is the gift of God—not by works, so that no one can boast."* (Ephesians 2:8 & 9) He told me I just needed to have faith, which was right, but I kept thinking it was something that I needed to do to get God to save me. He didn't tell me it was a gift from God that I just needed to accept. Please understand, I am not blaming my uncle. He was trying to help me the best he knew how and I appreciate all the ways and means that my family church tried to help me by teaching me about God and by setting a good example for me. It might have been easier if someone had been able to explain to me from the scriptures how I could be saved but fortunately God is able to take care of the task in spite of what others can, or can't, or do or don't do. Once again, it proves to be very important for Christians to read the direction manual for our lives so we can lead others in the right way. We don't want to only know the way ourselves, we want to be able to help others find it even if we cannot explain it exactly in detail.

I do not think it was at that service but at one some time later that the Holy Spirit filled my heart in such a way that for a few seconds I felt as light as a feather, almost like I was lifted off my feet. I do know that after that incident, I never once again doubted that I was saved. It is truly a blessed feeling to know that your sins are forgiven and you are a child of the King. Jesus said in John 8:31 & 32 (NIV) *"If you hold to my teaching, you are really my disciples. Then you will know the truth, and the truth will set you free."*

It is a wonderful thing for our spirit to be free. Free to learn, to experience, to grow into the person God intended us to be from the time we were conceived in our mother's womb. My free spirit gave me this poem.

My Saviour

Free to see your beauty all around me,
Free to hear your voice 'ore land and sea.
Free to fathom thoughts that astound me,
Free to know a God such as thee.

Remind me often of the bonds that held me,
The gripping fetters tight around my soul,
The pain I felt from weights heavy upon me,
When sin like chains upon my spirit hold.

I was lost as stars without a galaxy,
No hope of being found was there for me,
You were there to put your arms around me,
To free me from my sins and set me free!

Different scriptures in the Bible say that people were chosen by God for a specific purpose, even before they were conceived, such as Abraham, Samuel and John the Baptist. I don't believe he loves each of us any less or treats us any differently. In Jeremiah 29:11-13, (NIV) he says, *"For I know the plans I have for you, "declares the Lord, "plans to prosper you and not to harm you, plans to give you hope and a future. Then you will call upon me and come and pray to me, and I will listen to you. You will seek me and find me when you seek me with all your heart."* Isn't that awesome, just to think that even before we were conceived, we were in God's plans!

After all my searching, to this day, I believe that if a person will truly seek God with all their heart, one way or another they will find Him because He is also seeking for us. He would not be a loving God if this were not true, would He?

ANOTHER GENERATION

During the years that our children were growing up, each experienced their own conversion, was baptized and joined the church. We continued to attend and support the church faithfully. My husband was ordained a deacon and I worked willingly in whatever capacity I could.

My cousin, Margie (Madison) Littrell and I organized and started the first Vacation Bible School our church had ever had. We visited in the community surrounding the church, inviting any children that wanted to come, provided their parents would allow them. It was hard for me to understand at the time that one family who were dedicated Christians and attended their church faithfully did not believe in Sunday school or Vacation Bible School and would not allow their children to attend. I believe their reasoning was that they felt Christians should be led only by the Holy Spirit and not be taught the Bible by others. They were very sincere in this conviction and I had to accept that even if I did not agree with it.

We provided transportation by arranging for teachers to pick up the children that lived on the route they traveled themselves. I remember hauling a load of children in the back of our light blue Chevrolet pickup that had wooden cattle racks on it. I transported several children this way and never had an incident. I'm sure that would not be allowed today. It was also the first time African Americans (they were called colored people then) were invited to share in the church services of our all white congregation. There was a little bit of opposition at a business meeting when we told them that they had been invited, but nothing major. We did not hesitate to invite them, but after thinking about it, decided maybe we should tell the church so there would be no surprises. I guess that is how the Holy Spirit works. There is no better unifying and equalizing force than the Holy Spirit. I really believe it works better in our society today than trying to make us 'politically correct' by legalization.

I think it was Abraham Lincoln who said, "The way to get rid of our enemies is to make friends of them." By the same token, I believe "The way to solve the racial problems is to make real Christians out of everybody."

The Vacation Bible Schools were well attended and quite successful for several years. So much so that one year we decided to have it for two weeks instead of one since the literature we used was written for two weeks and it seemed a waste not to use all of it. It was a good thing to try, but it proved too great a challenge. The kids seemed to like it fine but the teachers were totally exhausted. We didn't try it anymore but I don't think the church has missed having a VBS every summer to this day. A few years later the church where the black children (that we had invited to come) attended, started having their own VBS. Every good thing must have a beginning and it is encouraging to think that maybe one had a small part in it.

We also had a Christmas play for our special program during the holiday season. They were fun to do and the kids were given the opportunity to perform in front of people which was a good experience for them. I directed them for several years and even wrote a play for them on one occasion. It was always a challenge and hopefully reminded everyone of what the season was really about. I truly desired that would be the end result.

MY BELIEF CHALLENGED

In my early thirties there were two young girls by the name of Pam and Marlene that had visited another kind of church and they came to me asking questions that I could not answer. My immediate answer to them was, "Be careful and don't be misled. The Bible speaks a lot about false doctrine." I suppose this was the answer I had heard given before when people had questions about doctrine and other churches that were difficult to answer.

Many committed Christians are dedicated to the church they have membership in and attend regularly. It is not an uncommon practice to attend the same church all their life, or at least the same kind of church. They depend on the pastor and other leaders to teach them what they need to know. To my dismay, I am afraid that very few believers search out the truths for themselves or even question what they have been taught until that belief is threatened. I dare say if a poll was taken to see how many church members in all denominations have read and studied the whole bible it would be a small percentage. One might object that surely we can trust our pastor. In most cases, I believe we can, but we must remember that all men and women are human and capable of error. (Remember Jim Jones in Guyana) It also helps to keep us from putting our trust in them instead of God, who is the only one trustworthy. Remember, only Jesus can save us by entering our hearts via the Holy Spirit.

On the other hand, we might question the idea of parents teaching their children to follow their faith so strongly that it is akin to 'brainwashing.' The Bible does instruct his people to do this in Deuteronomy 6: 4-9. (NIV) It says, *"Hear, O Israel: The Lord our God, the Lord is one. Love the Lord your God with all your heart and with all your soul and with all your strength. These commandments that I give you today are to be upon your hearts. Impress them on your children. Talk about them when you sit at home and when you walk along the road, when you lie down and when you get up. Tie them as symbols on your hands and bind them on your foreheads. Write them on the doorframes of your houses and on your gates."*

Children need this guidance until they are older and can think things through for themselves. That is the purpose for parents. It would be a terrible catastrophe should we lead them in the wrong direction because we had not searched out the truth fully for ourselves.

I heard a story one time about a father who told his friend that in order to not 'brainwash' his children in their belief about religious things that he wasn't going to teach them anything and let them decide for themselves when they got old enough. The friend invited the father to walk with him out to his garden that was behind the house. As they approached one could immediately see that this was no garden, it was only a crop of weeds. If there was anything planted in it there was no evidence that the eye could see, and for sure, it would be crowded out by the weeds and produce nothing worthwhile. The father looked at his friend in amusement and said, "Do you call that a garden?" The friend replied, "Well, I did not want to interfere with nature so I just planted it and left it alone to see what it would produce." The father was astute enough to get the point.

It is, of course, a good thing to trust our parents but I am convinced that to truly believe something we have to make it our own. It is very good for parents to *'train up their children in the ways of the Lord'*. Proverbs 22: 6 promises if we do this that they will not depart from it when they are old. It does not promise that they will never question it. In fact, I think to question it is probably a necessity. If we do not consider carefully what we have been taught and determine if we believe it is truth or not, we are only taking someone else's word for deciding the most important thing in our life and in the hereafter.

I'm afraid that many, or maybe even most, people of faith are prone to be narrow in their thinking. I suppose this is because they sincerely believe they are right and need to look no further. I do not think this is a good thing. All protestant denominations base their doctrinal beliefs on the scriptures but each is also tempted to emphasize the part that they like best, or have been taught more ardently, and focus less on the rest. There are some that have their Bibles underlined or colored coded to point out their special emphasis.   This is one of the reasons there is sometimes disunity among churches of different denominations. The consensus of the majority knows only what the focus of their church is and if another churches' doctrine does not agree with theirs, they see the other as less than right. Let's say that Presbyterians believe strongly in education, Methodist love good singing, The Church of Christ promotes bible study, Catholics, Lutherans and others use many scriptural rituals and traditions, Assembly of God people love seeing the gifts of the spirit in operation and Baptists focus on good morals and works. There is nothing wrong with any of these things, in fact, they are all very right. Just think how much better it would be if all Christians promoted all of them. Since they are all scriptural I don't see how we can not do this. It would be interesting and exciting to see how the church (meaning all true Christians) would change our world if this could happen. It might be a repeat of the Book of Acts.

Let me return to my two young friends who came to me with questions. The questions came about because they (not me, I was too busy and dedicated to attending mine) had visited another church that was different than the one they usually attended. Their questions got my attention, especially the one concerning Acts 8: 15-17. They said, "What is the difference in being baptized in the name of the Lord Jesus and being baptized in the Holy Spirit?" I did not know, so I began to search for answers.

I had a large book called 'The Layman's Bible Encyclopedia, compiled by William C. Martin and published by The Southwestern Company of Nashville, Tennessee.' I have frequently commented that it is the only thing I ever bought from a door to door salesman that was worth the money.

I took it from my library shelf and looked up the word 'spirit.' It gave the main references in the Bible containing this word. I read and studied and reread these passages. I looked them up in the Bible and read the surrounding verses to make sure I was not taking them out of context. The more I learned, the more excited I became. How could I have missed something that was such a vital part of what being a Christian is all about? I saw how the Holy Spirit was present in the beginning of Genesis when the world was created and many times throughout the Old Testament at significant times. It was what had inspired the authors to write its thirty nine books.

In the New Testament it was even more important. I especially liked reading the book of Luke because he was a good storyteller and told things in detail. (Women like details!) He (the Holy Spirit) was there when Mary, a virgin, became pregnant with the Son of God. He was there when Elizabeth and Zacharias, who were past the age of child bearing, conceived a son and was told to name him John who would be the one to inform the world of the coming Messiah. It seemed everywhere the Holy Spirit appeared, miraculous things happened.

One of the most important parts was in John, chapters 14 & 15 where Jesus told his disciples he was going away so that the Holy Spirit could come and be everywhere at the same time. He explained how lives would be changed when people welcomed him into their heart. His explanation in found in John, chapter 3.

Although Jesus told them all about the Holy Spirit, the disciples did not understand completely what he meant. It was not until after Jesus ascended into heaven and they went back to Jerusalem and began their continuous prayer meeting as Jesus had instructed them to do that they understood. There were 120 people and they prayed for ten days before the Holy Spirit arrived as Jesus had promised. His presence was seen and felt by everyone there. The disciple, Peter, who had been such a coward a few days before at Jesus arrest, now stood and boldly proclaimed the name of Jesus and told the people, point blank, that they had crucified the very Son of God. It was a glorious time. All of the disciples were 'filled with the Holy Spirit' and began to speak in other tongues. There were people there from many foreign places who spoke various languages. The miracle was they all understood what the disciples were saying in their own language. Most were utterly amazed and perplexed and some, as usual, were critical. The critics made fun of them and accused them of having had too much wine. In spite of this it was a happy time. Thousands believed and received this Holy Spirit into their hearts and were added to the Kingdom of God on earth.

This was the beginning of the church. The entire book of Acts tells about the trials and triumphs of its organization and progress. It focuses on the ministries of Peter and Paul and how the Holy Spirit worked in their lives to accomplish great things for God. It is an inspiring and heart warming record of how God orchestrated the development of a people for himself here on His earth. It is a must read for any new Christian, or old one either, for that matter!

The rest of the New Testament bears record of how other churches were established and added. Each group of people who seek to follow these guidelines today is an extension of those churches. The thrilling part is that the Holy Spirit that we read about in the beginning of the church is still available today. He is just the same, just as powerful, just as able to teach us what is truth, convict us of our sins and encourage and help us overcome when we need help. The bible says all we need to do is ask. (Luke 11: 9-13.)

Why?

Why do birds sing?
Why do eagles fly?
Because they're different
From you and I!

Why do flowers bloom?
Why do Honeybees hum?
Because their work
Has just begun!

Why do snowflakes melt?
Why do raindrops fall?
Because of gravity
For one and all!

How can a whale swim?
Or lightning streak the sky?
Because God wills it
And that's no lie!

Why do I wonder?
Why do I sigh?
Because God is bigger
Than you and I!

THE BIBLE IS EXCITING

This newfound knowledge of the work of the Holy Spirit in the world and in the lives of Christians down thru the ages made me want to know more. I read the Book of Acts and I asked for this Holy Spirit that it talked about. I did not hear bells ringing, I did not speak in another tongue or do anything else that was out of the ordinary (that is not to say that other people may have this experience) but I was given a desire to read the Bible to search out its truths. I wanted to know what else it said that I was unaware of. I remember my husband asking me one day when I was reading it if a person could read the Bible too much. I don't know what my answer was but one thing I do know is that the opposite is true. One can fail to read the Bible enough. So many people think that it is a bunch of dos and don'ts and do not want those restrictions in their lives. If you read only the old law in the books of Leviticus and Deuteronomy you would surely get this idea but if you do not stop there and read the rest of it you learn that this is not true. You will find instead, that it is a guide for our lives to help us avoid the pitfalls that will hinder us from living life in its fullness. Jesus said in John 10:10, *"The thief (Satan) came to steal, kill and destroy but I am come that he might have life and have it abundantly."*(KJV) It is here in all the pages of this book that we learn the secret for this kind of life.

One might compare the Bible to a motherboard. I only know what that is because one of our exchange students from Germany was a whiz at computers. His father's occupation was creating motherboards for computers. He knew the intricate workings of all the little wires and tiny parts that it contained and what each one played in making the computer do all the wonderfully complex things it can do. He was the one that wrote the instructions on how to put it together for it to work perfectly. Because of this, there was nothing that could be wrong with a computer that he could not fix. He also knew how to keep it running smoothly day after day.

Since God is the one who created us, mind, body and spirit, he also is the one who knows best how to make us work without complications. We are the motherboard and would be wise to follow his instructions. I am not the best at directions so I need a good map or a GPS when I am going somewhere and do not know the way. While searching the scriptures I found just that. The Holy Spirit gave me a desire to know and helped me to understand the directions. He (the Holy Spirit) is always there and I keep a Bible handy because I often lose my way and need help. If both the Holy Spirit and the Word agree it is my confirmation that it is the right thing to do.

In addition to using the Bible as a map for direction in our lives, it is also an interesting and amazing book. I have heard many people say that it is hard to read, not interesting and that they cannot understand it. This may have something to do with their motivation for reading it. If it is from a sense of duty because they think they should to be a 'good' Christian, it probably will be difficult to understand. If it is to compete in a Bible drill by knowing the answer to the most questions, that may be all one will accomplish. If it is to argue with someone over whose religion is right and whose is wrong, the benefits may be few. If it is to read the Bible through so we can brag about it, God is probably not impressed.

In my own life I believe it was only when I read the

Bible, sincerely searching for answers that I found them. That is not to say that God cannot or will not use his word to draw people to himself even when they may be reading it for the wrong reason. Remember, he rarely does things the same way. He made us all different and he knows how best to get our attention. The way we find Him may be different than others. In spite of this, I believe that one day He will accomplish his purpose of bringing us all together in unity as was his prayer in John 17. I repeat, "The Holy Spirit is the most unifying organism I know." I can only imagine what it would do for our governmental system if applied!"

The amazing part about the Bible is that it was written over an approximate 1500 year span of time, by over 40 different authors and yet it conveys one central message throughout. I'm sure there are many different ways to say it and not be wrong, but I like to think that it was written to help God's creation (us) become people who will bring honor and glory to him and his name. It is much the same principle as a parent wanting their children to become the kind of people they can be proud of and who shows them love and appreciation. We also want our children to be happy and know that the two go hand in hand. Jesus said in Matthew 6: 33, (KJV) *"Seek ye first the kingdom of God and his righteousness and all these other things will be added."* This has always proved to be a good rule to live by. It might surprise you that when you seek God and his righteousness first, how few other things you will desperately need or desire.

There are many ways to read the Bible and all of them are good. I did a thorough study of the bible one time with the aid of a book entitled 'What the Bible Says' by Henrietta Mears. It was a great help to me. I did not read it in the order the books came. I read it by individual books. Before I would read a book I would read the outline given by Ms. Mears. It told who wrote the book and when, where, why, and how to watch for the main points that the writer was making. Sometimes I would read an entire book at one setting. It is just like meeting a friend and getting to know them.

Historians have divided the Bible up in categories. The first five books in the Old Testament are called the law or the Pentateuch; the next ten are history; Esther, Job, Psalms, Proverbs, Ecclesiastes, Song of Solomon and Lamentations are know as poetry; the five books of Nehemiah, Isaiah, Jeremiah, Ezekiel and Daniel are called the major prophets simply because they are more lengthy, and the rest of the Old Testament books (12 of them) are minor prophets because they are short. (This was Ms. Mear's version. Others may differ to some degree and that is no problem as far as I am concerned.)

In the following list I will give you a little information about each book that is mostly taken from the New International version of the Bible. The name of the person listed at the end of each is the main character in that book.

THE 'LAW' OR 'CANON'

- GENESIS - means beginning - explains the beginning of the universe, earth, people, sin and God's plan for salvation. - MOSES

- EXODUS - means 'to exit' - the exodus of God's people from slavery (sin) in Egypt - MOSES

- LEVITICUS - a form of the word 'Levi'. The priests who were in charge of the religious activities were from the tribe of Levi. The laws for God's people to live by are listed in this book. - MOSES

- NUMBERS - a 'census' (counting numbers) taken of God's people in order to organize them in preparation for entering the Promised Land – MOSES

- DEUTERONOMY - 'duet' meaning 'two' - to remind God's people by repeating the second time what he had done for them and what they had promised Him. - MOSES AND JOSHUA

BOOKS OF HISTORY

- JOSHUA - a history of conquering the Promised Land - JOSHUA

- JUDGES - history of the fifteen judges that ruled Israel between Joshua and Saul – SAMUEL (possibly)

- RUTH - traces the ancestry of David to Ruth and presents a beautiful picture of piety and its' rewards from Ruth and her mother-in-law, Naomi. (a love story) - RUTH

- I & II SAMUEL- history of the Israelites' first king, Saul, and second one, David - SAMUEL (mainly)

- I & II KINGS - history of the kings of the southern and northern kingdoms of Israel - UNKNOWN (JEREMIAH or A GROUP OF PROPHETS)

- I & II CHRONICLES - history of Israel through genealogies of kings, prophets, leaders, priests, etc. – EZRA

- EZRA - to show that God is faithful to keep his promises – EZRA

MAJOR PROPHET

- NEHEMIAH - history of the return to Jerusalem after captivity and the rebuilding of the wall – NEHEMIAH

POETRY

- ESTHER - story of Esther (Hadassah) and how God used her to save the Jewish people - UNKNOWN (possibly MORDECAI, EZRA, OR NEHEMIAH)

- JOB - Job's story of being tested and God's sovereignty - UNKNOWN (possibly MOSES, SOLOMON or ELIHU)

- PSALMS - poems of praise, worship and confession to God – DAVID (mainly), ASAPH, SONS OF KORAH, SOLOMON, HEMAN, ETHAN AND MOSES (51 are unknown)

- PROVERBS - to provide wisdom and moral instruction for daily life -- SOLOMON (mainly), AGUR and LEMUEL

- ECCLESIASTES - to teach us the true meaning of life - SOLOMON

- SONG OF SOLOMON - to teach us about real love and marriage – SOLOMON

MAJOR PROPHETS

- ISAIAH -to call the nation of Judah back to God and tell of God's salvation through the Messiah - ISAIAH

- JEREMIAH - to urge God's people to turn from their sins and back to God and of the coming destruction if they did not - JEREMIAH (known as the weeping prophet)

POETRY

- LAMENTATIONS - to teach us that disobedience brings suffering to us and God - JEREMIAH

MAJOR PROPHETS

- EZEKIEL - to tell Israel and other nations of their coming judgment and foretell the eventual salvation of God's people - EZEKIEL

- DANIEL - history of the faithful Jews while in captivity, including himself - DANIEL

MINOR PROPHETS

- HOSEA - to illustrate God's love for his sinful people by Hosea's marriage to his wife, Gomer - HOSEA

(In the following books the scripture quotations listed following each book is one of my favorite ones in that book. I have included it to help me identify with it since the Minor Prophets are not the most read books of the bible.)

- <u>JOEL</u> - to warn Judah of God's judgment because of their sins and urge them to return to God - JOEL
"And afterward, I will pour out my Spirit on all people. Your sons and daughters will prophesy, your old men will dream dreams, and your young men will see visions." 2:28(NIV)

- <u>AMOS</u> - to pronounce God's judgment on Israel (the northern kingdom) because of their evil doings - AMOS (Amos was an itinerate preacher, a herder of sheep and a gatherer of sycamore fruit (a farmer)
"But let justice roll on like a river, and righteousness as a mighty stream!"5:24(KJV)

- <u>OBADIAH</u> - to show that God judges those who have harmed his people – OBADIAH (little known about him) (He spoke frequently about 'the day of the Lord')
"The day of the Lord is near for all nations. As you have done, it will be done to you; your deeds will return upon your own head." 1:15 (NIV) (only one chapter)

- <u>JONAH</u> - to reveal God's grace by the story of the whale & Jonah - JONAH

- <u>MICAH</u> - to warn God's people that judgment is coming and to offer pardon to all who repent - MICAH (He prophesied that Jesus would be born in Bethlehem) Ch 5:2
"He has showed you, O man, what is good. And what does the Lord require of you? To act justly and to love mercy and to walk humbly with your God."6:7&8 (NIV)

- <u>NAHUM</u> - to pronounce God's judgment on Nineveh and Assyria and comfort Judah with this truth - NAHUM (very colorful writing about God being sovereign and in control, making justice ultimately reign)

- HABAKKUK - to show that God is still in control of the world despite the apparent triumph of evil - HABAKKUK *"But the Lord is in his holy temple; let all the earth be silent before him."2:20 (NIV)*

- ZEPHANIAH - to shake the people of Judah out of their complacency and urge them to return to God - ZEPHANIAH (talked a lot about the 'day of the Lord')

- HAGGAI - to call the people to complete the rebuilding of the temple HAGGAI *"Is it a time for you yourselves to be living in your paneled houses, while God's house remains a ruin?"1:4 (NIV)*

- ZECHARIAH - to give God's people hope by revealing God's future deliverance through the Messiah - ZECHARIAH *"Not by might, nor by power, but by my Spirit, says the Lord of Hosts."4:6 (KJV)*

- MALACHI - to confront the people with their sins and to restore their relationship with God - MALACHI (Also verses concerning tithing and marriage) *"Surely the day is coming; it will burn like a furnace . . .But for you who revere my name, the sun of righteousness will rise with healing in its wings, And you will go out and leap like calves released from the stall" 4:1&2 (NIV)*

In the New Testament, the first four books that tell about the life of Jesus while he was on earth are called the gospels. The book of ACTS is considered 'history,' Revelation is known as 'prophesy' and the other twenty one books are called 'letters' or 'espistles' because that is what they were. Ms. Mears tells us that each of the gospels and many of the letters were written by the person bearing its name and all were written for a different reason. I suppose that is why they were all included in the canon.

THE GOSPELS

- MATTHEW - written by MATTHEW - (also called LEVI) _ Matthew, who was a Jew by birth, wrote his gospel to the Jewish people to convince them that Jesus was the Messiah, the eternal King that they had been waiting and looking for. He did this by recording many of the prophetic verses from the Old Testament about this Messiah and showing them how Jesus fulfilled those prophesies. The Jewish people expected the Messiah, that was to come, would set up His kingdom on earth and that is the way He is portrayed by Matthew - as a king. This is one of the reasons he begins his book with the genealogy of Jesus via King David. To royalty, genealogies are very important. Matthew was one of the twelve disciples that Jesus chose to be with him during his earthy ministry. From the status of a despised tax collector to a child of the king, he had experienced first hand, and knew without a doubt, that Jesus was who He said He was. It is only natural that when we experience Jesus in our heart and know for sure who He is, we want others to know too.

- MARK - written by MARK - Mark was a young man when Jesus was on earth. Some writers believe he must have been about the age of fifteen to seventeen. It is not hard to imagine being an active, curious and inquisitive teenager and finding all of the goings-on, wherever Jesus was, quite interesting and intriguing.

According to my revered encyclopedia, Mark was a Palestinian Jew named John. Mark was his Roman name. He must have had a special interest in the Romans because that is to whom he writes. They were people who believed in action. They did not just sit around and talk about something, they did it. Mark portrays Jesus as a person of action and one who could make a difference in one's life. He also presented him as a servant. His book is full of miracles and parables with Jesus ministering to people everywhere he went. Mark was later a missionary. Many believe that his book was the first gospel that was written.

- <u>LUKE</u> – written by LUKE - As I stated earlier, I like the Book of Luke because of it's allegiance to detail. Luke was a doctor, or physician, if you prefer, (Colossians 4: 14) a Greek and a Gentile Christian. In fact, he is the only known Gentile author in the New Testament. He also wrote the book of Acts, which is a continuation of Luke. He wrote both books for his friend Theophilus, and to Gentiles. Being an educated man of science and a Greek who were known for their interest in philosophy, Luke writes of his affirmation of the divinity of Jesus as well as his humanity. He leaves no doubt that God was the divine father of Jesus and Mary was his earthly mother. He portrays him as the Son of God and also the Son of man. He begins his book by stating that he has done his research, carefully investigating everything from the beginning and will give an orderly account of all the facts surrounding Jesus so that we may know for sure what is true. He does just that, beginning with the birth of John the Baptist, who was to introduce Jesus to the world, all the way through His life and ascension into heaven. He stops his first book immediately following Jesus ascension and takes up where he left off with a short review in the first chapter of Acts.

- JOHN– written by JOHN - The first three gospels, Matthew, Mark and Luke are known as the synoptic gospels meaning they are the same story with a slightly different account from each writer. The fourth gospel, the book of John is about Jesus also, but it is written from an entirely different point of view. John's purpose in writing it was to convince people, without a doubt, that Jesus really was who he said he was, the Son of God. He tells us how his power can make a difference in our lives now and eternally. It is an especially good read for new Christians or older ones who are questioning their faith. At different times he asked people straight out, who did they think Jesus was. He also lists many of the major miracles to prove his point. John was what some people today would call an intuitive person. I believe he was more in connection with his spiritual nature than the other gospel writers. He knew Jesus on a more intimate level because his thinking went deeper than just the physical realm. He includes Jesus telling them about the Holy Spirit and the part he plays in the life of his followers. At one point in the story about the woman at the well, Jesus said, *"The time will come when they that worship God must worship him in spirit and in truth."* (Chapter 4) After Jesus died on the cross, arose, ascended back to the Father and sent the Holy Spirit, that promise was fulfilled. The time he spoke of had arrived, and is now here. This is the reason we must worship God 'in the spirit' (honestly and sincerely from our heart) and not just repeat or perform rituals in order to relate to God. John also wrote the three short books of I, II and III John and the last book in the New Testament which is

'Revelation.' In the beginning of the book of Revelation it says, 'John was in the spirit on the Lord's Day' and he was instructed to write down the things he saw. This is another instance that shows the special relationship that John had with the Trinity. (God, Jesus and Holy Spirit) John was the brother of James, another disciple. Zebedee was their father and the two were called "Sons of Thunder."

HISTORY

- ACTS - written by LUKE - The Book of Acts is considered to be the history section of the New Testament. It tells about the beginning of the Church (kingdom of God) on earth and how it spread quickly to other parts of the world. I have already stated that Luke was the writer and you will notice it is very detailed and factual. The two main characters are Peter and Paul who God used in mighty ways because they were willing to allow the Holy Spirit to work through them. I loved reading it when searching for understanding of the Holy Spirit in my own life. It is a great reference to use when convincing people of no or little faith that the Bible is truly God's message to us.

LETTERS

The next twenty one books are called 'the letters or epistles. Paul wrote the first nine of them to the churches he had helped establish by the same name as the book. His purpose was to instruct and encourage them in their relationships with other Christians and in the development of the church.

- ROMANS - written by PAUL to the Christians in Rome and Christians everywhere - to present himself to the Romans before arriving there and give a statement of his faith and message

- I CORINTHIANS - written by PAUL to the church in Corinth - there were many problems in the church in Corinth and Paul wrote to instruct them as to how to live for Christ in a corrupt society.

- II CORINTHIANS - written by PAUL - to the church in Corinth - to defend his authority in Christ and refute the teachings of false prophets in their midst

- GALATIANS - written by PAUL to the churches in southern Galatia - to teach them about faith and freedom in Christ.

- EPHESIANS - written by PAUL to the church at Ephesus - to encourage the believers at Ephesus in their faith and explain the nature and purpose of the church as the body of Christ.

- PHILIPPIANS - written by PAUL to the Christians at Philippi - to thank them for their gift and teach them about true joy

- COLLOSIANS - written by PAUL to the church at Colosse - to combat errors in the church and help them understand that they have everything they need in Christ (I love the prayer in Chapter 1.)

- I THESSALONIANS - written by PAUL to the church at Thessalonica - to encourage them and assure them of Christ's return

- <u>II THESSALONIANS -</u> written by PAUL to the church at Thessalonica - to clear up confusion about the second coming of Christ

- <u>I TIMOTHY</u> - written by PAUL to Timothy and young church leaders - to give encouragement and instruction to Timothy who was like a son to him

- <u>II TIMOTHY</u> - written by PAUL to Timothy - to give more encouragement and instruction to Timothy who was pastor of the church at Ephesus

- <u>TITUS</u> - written by PAUL to Titus, a Greek convert, - to advise Titus in his responsibility of supervising the churches on the island of Crete

- <u>PHILEMON</u> - written by PAUL to Philemon, who was probably a wealthy member of the Colossian church - to convince him to forgive Onesimus, his runaway slave, and to accept him back as a brother in the faith.

- <u>HEBREWS -</u> the author is unknown, PAUL, LUKE, BARNABAS, APOLLOS, SILAS, PHILIP and others have been suggested - written to the Hebrew Christians - to present the sufficiency and superiority of Christ.

- <u>JAMES</u> - written by JAMES, who was Jesus' brother and a leader in the Jerusalem church, to the Jewish Christians outside Palestine - to expose hypocritical practices and to teach right Christian behavior.

- <u>I PETER</u> - written by PETER to Jewish Christians driven out of Jerusalem and scattered throughout Asia Minor - to offer encouragement in suffering

- <u>II PETER</u> - written by PETER to all churches and believers of that time - to warn them about false teachers and exhort them to grow in their faith in and knowledge of Christ

- <u>I JOHN</u> - written by the apostle JOHN to several Gentile congregations and all believers of that time - to reassure Christians in their faith and to counter false teachings

- <u>II JOHN</u> - written by the apostle JOHN to 'the chosen lady' and her children (possibly to a local church), and other believers of that time - to warn against false teachers and emphasize that the basics of following Christ are truth and love

- <u>III JOHN</u> - written by the apostle JOHN to Gaius, a prominent Christian in one of the churches known to John, to commend Gaius for his hospitality and to encourage him in his Christian life

- <u>JUDE</u> - written by JUDE, brother of Jesus and James, to Jewish Christians and all believers of that time - to remind the church of the need for constant vigilance, to keep strong in the faith and to oppose heresy

PROPHESY

- <u>REVELATION</u> - written by the apostle JOHN to the seven churches in Asia and all believers of that time - to reveal the full identity of Christ and to give warning and hope to believers.

As I wrote earlier, Revelation was written by the disciple John while he was on an island called Patmos.

He had been exiled there as punishment for his testimony of Jesus and the word of God. The seven churches he wrote the letters to were Ephesus, Symrna, Pergamum, Thyatira, Sardis, Philadelphia, and Laodicea. I have an idea that they are representative of all churches today. Each is described and none are alike.

The rest is a vision that John wrote about and he explained it in symbols. He referred to Christ's second coming and described what heaven will be like. I think the book is a bit difficult to understand but I also think we should read and study it. If it had not been important it would not have been included in the New Testament. The one overpowering thought I get from Revelation each time I read it is that I sure do want to be on God's side. I guess that is enough reason to read it often.

Much of the above information on the books of the bible was taken from The New International Bible. It also states that these letters of the New Testament were inspired by the Holy Spirit to be written for all Christians everywhere during the period they were written and since. They are as applicable for Christians today as they were then.

I feel I have profited from reading the Bible in different versions and translations. One year I purchased a paperback 'one year' Bible. It was written with a specific text beginning in Genesis 1, a small portion from Psalms or Proverbs, and a reading from the New Testament, for each day of the year. At the end of the year I had read the whole Bible. It was an interesting and rewarding way to read it. I do not remember who compiled it and do not have it to reference because I passed it on to someone else. I do remember that I did not always read every specific passage that was recommended for every day but I would 'catch up' periodically. It was good motivation to complete the entire book and anytime we read it, no matter when, how, where or what version, we gain wisdom that is unattainable from any other source.

Another year I chose to read 'The Daily Bible' In Chronological Order – 365 Daily Readings in the New International Version. It had commentary by F. LaGard Smith that was very good. I liked the idea of it being written in the order that it happened and, again, the one year layout was a good guide to go by.

I am in the process of reading the Life Application Study Bible in the New International Version. It has many extra helps and good information that I am also reading as I go. Last year I joined Bible Study Fellowship and found it to be a good way to study the Bible with other Christian women. I connect the two studies together and find that it works quite well.

In John 1:1, it says *"In the beginning was the Word and the Word was with God and the Word was God."* (KJV) Later on in that same chapter in verse 14 it says, *"The Word became flesh and dwelt among us."* (KJV) I am convinced that Jesus is the way, the truth and the life as it says in John 14:6, and in the Bible is the Word that shows us the way to that life with God. Luke 21:33 says, *"Heaven and earth shall pass away but my Word shall not pass away."* Surely many have tried to do away with it but there are more Bibles today than at any time in history. The sad part is that we don't read it and use it.

Once I learned to love God's word, the motivation to read it was not hard to come by. It is nourishment for my spiritual body like food is for my physical body. Many years ago the Holy Spirit revealed to me just how important this is.

In my early years as a believer I struggled with the difference between my ideas and those of others about what being a Christian is all about. I have already expressed how the church we attended stressed exceptionally good morals and committed church attendance. There were other churches in nearby communities that were a different denomination and they focused on having a two or three week revival once a year with many people saved or renewed in their faith. They were very spirit filled, emotional services and the attendance from their members and other same denominational churches nearby was tremendous. The problem, in my opinion, was that the everyday life of these members of the same faith, different denomination, was many times lacking in good morals and church attendance. They usually only had church services one Saturday night and the following Sunday in each month. Some had a small attendance for Sunday school (Bible Study) and some did not believe in having Bible Study. (This was because they believed that one should be led solely by the Spirit.) Growing up, these two different denominations were the only ones I knew much about (They were two kinds of Baptist) and the Church of Christ to which one of my aunt and uncle's family attended. My only concept of this church was 'They thought they were the only ones who were right.' Here again, the focus was on what we disagreed on instead of what we agreed on. At that time, I had never attended either of these different kinds of churches, thus, my knowledge was only hearsay. However, my desire to understand the difference was very real. When I married someone that had grown up in the other kind of Baptist Church, the problem became even larger. Tom, my husband's family's church was not as extreme in their doctrine and practices as many of the others I knew of and that was advantageous for us. We would take turns going to his church and then to mine for several years. Probably since mine had a larger and regular attendance we chose to attend there. Tom joined the church where I had attended and he later became a deacon. We faithfully attended as a family during our boys growing up years. Through it all, I constantly searched for answers to understand why there were such differences.

Early one morning, as I lay in bed in a kind of half sleep, this revelation came to me 'as clear as a bell.' I was not even thinking about it at the time and I did not hear it audibly but it was a completely new idea that I had never contemplated before.

These are the thoughts that came to me.

Our spiritual bodies are much like our physical bodies. They need nourishment to keep them healthy. If we were to eat only one huge meal a week, no matter how many good vitamins and minerals it had in it, we would get weak and hungry before our next meal. Because of this, it is better to eat balanced meals each day, even three times a day, and spread out the different kinds of foods from all the four food groups. Our bodies are much more likely to stay, vibrant, healthy and well and serve us effectively. We look better, feel better and enjoy living to a greater capacity if we stay nourished.

Our spiritual bodies are the same except we substitute worship for food. If we only feed them one huge meal on Sunday or our Sabbath by whatever means they are nourished and neglect them for the rest of the week, they are going to become weak and of no pleasure or use to us or God most of the time. They need food on a regular basis just like our bodies and they flourish when we provide different kinds of foods for them. One of the spiritual foods I most hunger for is the Bible. It is amazing how the word of God soothes my troubled spirit, provides guidance and strengthens my faith. Other foods, for me, are playing or listening to inspiring music, singing praises or listening to them, meditation, nature, prayer, reading, walking, etc. I exercise in my swimming pool in the summer and I love to worship there in sort of a dance song. Like physical foods, different people desire different foods. The secret is that we seek them regularly and take time to enjoy them and provide nourishment for our spiritual bodies. The taking time to enjoy them is an important part of the whole process. It provides health to our physical bodies as well.

I will never forget a lesson I learned from Victor, one of our exchange students from Brazil who lived with us for four and a half months. He was Latin, a very healthy and intelligent young man and a swimmer. One day we were coming from swimming practice and I stopped at a Mint Mart to pick up a deli sandwich for him. We had to be at another place shortly and since our schedule was running close I suggested that he could eat it on the way home. He was aghast. He said, "That's no way to eat. Food was once alive and deserves our respect. You are supposed to sit down at the table and enjoy eating it, slowly and with relish." He waited until we got home and did just that.

I'm glad I was wise enough to listen and take his advice. It is so much healthier and enjoyable to take time to enjoy both physical and spiritual food. After all, the good life is not a station we arrive at but the journey. I'm afraid many of us are missing this important point.

This idea can be extended further to include our mental and emotional bodies along with the physical and spiritual. They are all interconnected and what one does affects the other. If we are not healthy physically our mental and emotional bodies do not function as well either. If we think positively (mental body) we are more apt to be stronger emotionally and spiritually, etc. The example I like best is from the bible. Matthew 6: 33 (KJV) *"But, seek ye first the kingdom of God and his righteousness and all these other things will be added unto you."* I am convinced that when we keep our spiritual body healthy by making it our priority the others will function better also.

MEMORIES OF THE
OLD COUNTRY CHURCH

Ole' Buck and Charlie faithfully attended church. They not only went but pulled the old wooden wheeled wagon that took my family to worship every Sunday morning and any other time there were services at the small country church in the community where we lived when I was a little girl. Ole' Buck was a white mule, known for his stubbornness and adventurous enthusiasm. Charlie was a big, brown horse who was patient, steady and dependable. They were a good pair, kind of like a man and wife; totally opposite personalities but working together toward the same goal; they made a good team.

One of my first and fondest memories was riding to church in that wagon with my three older siblings between quilts on a bed of straw to keep us warm. The weather was cold but that didn't keep us from going to church. Mama and Daddy rode up front on the buckboard that was a seat on springs. The springs added bounce over the rough, dirt road we traveled to get there. Bricks, heated in the fireplace before we left, were placed under and around their feet to keep them warm. It was only a little over a mile to the church so the short distance was a positive factor. I was young and can remember doing it only one time but knowing how dedicated my parents were to going to church, I'm sure we did it regularly.

The church was pretty much a family church; not by decree, because everyone was welcome, but most of the people who lived in the community were related as was often the case back then. My maternal great grandparents were charter members.

Another memory was the big pot-bellied wood/coal stove that sat in the middle of the church. Fires were built to heat the big room and keep us warm. The heat wasn't nearly as equally distributed as it is now with central heat and cooling. One side of us would be too hot, the other side too cold. Since everyone was used to it I don't remember hearing anyone complain.

I can remember the church being full and overflowing and the small children (that included me) having to sit on the step that went up to the pulpit in the front of the church. This happened mostly during revivals that were usually held in the spring and/or fall. I can remember my mother cleaning house and cooking big meals for our family and our pastor and his wife as well as the evangelist and his wife. It was a big occasion when 'the preacher came' and it happened quite often at our house. After I married, the tradition was continued and they came to our new home also. It was no small feat to get up on Sunday morning, prepare dinner and get our family ready in time for Sunday school and church at ten o'clock. I remember one pastor who had six children; that was eight plus our five! I would never shirk my responsibility though and 'feeding the preacher' was one of them. There was a 'preacher list' that contained all the names of the families who were willing to host the pastor when their time rolled around according to the list. The pastor never lived in the community, so when he came on Sunday for Sunday school and Church he went home with the designated family for dinner and stayed until church services that night. Looking back now I suppose it was a good way for the pastor to get to know his parishioners – at least the ones who would allow their name to be on 'the list.' I also remember Mama complaining about the women who would not allow their names to be on it. She had the largest family in the church and Mama thought if she could do it anybody could. She was probably right, and I doubt that she ever thought of herself as being judgmental . . . as many people would be quick to point out, especially today.

At revival time we sometimes held day services during the week or two weeks we had services at night. If someone doesn't know what a 'revival' is, it is having services every night and usually inviting an evangelist to come and preach for us. Many times our pastor and the evangelist took turns. Revivals were to revive us spiritually and also a time to encourage new people to become members and be added to the church by conversion and baptism. I can remember revivals when several people were 'saved' and I can also remember many times in my later years when no unsaved people even attended revivals or rarely any other time either.

My father worked at a factory and was gone in the daytime so we had to find a way to go to the day services. They were usually at ten or eleven o'clock in the mornings. One day I especially remember, because one of my cousins drove us in a car and we came close to   having a bad accident. The church sat on a hill.   We pulled into the church yard with the car headed down the hill. When she started to stop, the brakes either did not work or she got scared and forgot to pump them. We flew down the hill and stopped only when the car hit a big ditch in the corner of the two roads. It gave us a good scare.

Many churches still have revivals but in some it is a thing of the past. Because of cultural changes it may be something that has outgrown its usefulness. When the custom began it was because churches did not have full time pastors as most do today, and many people were illiterate or did not have their own Bibles. The services were held when the preacher was available. Before my lifetime was the era of the circuit riding preacher who traveled on horseback from church to church to hold services. My maternal grandfather, Richard Cecil Hardison, was this kind of preacher in the early part of his ministry.

Today the church I attend has many services through the week and the various pastor's offices are open most of the time. If anyone needs spiritual guidance or assistance it is available. On special occasions we might have two or three nights of service in a row to hear a specific speaker who travels a long distance to be with us. The travel is usually by airplane. That is quite a contrast to the days of the circuit riding preacher, isn't it? I guess that just illustrates an important point. The ways and means we use to worship God can and do change from generation to generation but the God we worship never changes. Hebrews 13:8 says, *"He is the same, yesterday, today and forever."* How reassuring and comforting to know that we can trust him and depend on the truths of his word no matter what comes or goes.

HISTORY OF THE COUNTRY CHURCH

Fairview General Baptist Church is the name of the church I attended the first thirty-five years of my life. It is a country church located on Highway 1339 which has been recently named Fairview Church Road. I can imagine that its' story is very similar to the story of most country churches.

Fairview Church held their 100th Anniversary in 2001. I wanted to share in their celebration so I wrote the following poem for the occasion. It reflects many of my sentiments and memories of my childhood that were connected with being a part of that century old institution.

Church on the Hill

I remember---
All day on Saturday, come what may;
We must prepare for the coming day.
The house to clean, wood to cut,
Water to haul, a hen to pluck;
A cake to bake, it must be done;
Baths to take-- lots of fun;
Hair to curl for the girls;
Trim and shaves for the boys;
Shoes polished, all in a row;
Ready for church, when time to go-

The sun is low, the day is spent;
We're all prepared, for the main event.
Sundays were made to go to church;
To sing and pray and put God first;
To honor His name the best we can;

To love and serve our fellow man;
To study the Bible and glorify God;
Listen to 'preachin,' trying not to nod!
It made its' mark; the roots sank deep;
Into our hearts; a harvest to reap-
God's word is true, it will not fail,
Even when troubles strongly assail;
The older I grow, the greater still.
I truly appreciate
The 'Church on the hill.'

In the foyer of the church, which I frequent quite often these days because my five siblings and I take turns caring for our mother who attends there, hangs a small framed document that shows when Fairview General Baptist Church was organized and who the charter members were. My mother is ninety-nine years old and in good health except for getting around with a walker and her memory is failing enough that we think she needs someone with her. We each alternate staying with her for twenty-four hour segments. She was born in 1910, and the church was organized six years earlier in 1904. She has gone to church there almost all of her life except for a year or so when she and my father lived in Louisville. My mother's grandfather, Richard C. Hardison was one of the organizers and he and his wife, Sarah George Hardison were also charter members. The church was located in the Rocky Hill-Sinking Springs community and a clerk and pastor were elected. Worship services were to be held on the 4th Saturday night and Sunday and Sunday school (Bible Study) every Sunday morning. A monthly business meeting was set for Saturday evening before the regular monthly services. The people met in the Sinking Springs School House for approximately a year. There was much interest and many of the neighbors attended.

In the spring of the following year the group decided they needed a building of their own and began to develop their vision. Mr. & Mrs. Morgan Mitchell (whose bones now lie in the small fenced cemetery near the present building) donated the plot of ground on which the church building was to be erected, and still is today. A beautiful hilltop site, bordered at that time by two main roads, and close to the community school, made it a good location. Three trustees were selected and the deed was made on the 2nd day of February, 1906.

As soon as the weather permitted, the men started cutting trees for logs to be made into lumber for the new church building. These trees were taken from the men's farms and given to further the Kingdom of God on earth. The whole trunks of strong, long and slender trees were used for the floor joists with large stones used at the corners and in between for the foundation. The framing and boxing were cut from the logs as was the majority of the material used. The men did almost all of the work themselves, using the tools they had at their disposal. Crosscut saws and axes were used for felling the trees. A sawmill turned them into lumber, and hand saws, hammers and nails were used to size and fit them into place. A tool known as a fro was used for making the wood shingles for the roofing. These were made from oak trees, whereas, poplar trees were cut and planed by hand for the weather boarding.

The interior of the building had a three foot high baseboard of beaded or tongue-grooved material, which ran all the way around. This same material was used for the ceiling. The walls were plastered and papered and the floor was made of oak planks about four inches wide.

The men made the seats out of 2x2 inch pieces of wood, except for the ends and middles of the benches which were ordered. They were called rail seats and were said to have been very uncomfortable. I think the phrase was 'they just simply cut your back in two."

As I stated earlier, the building was heated with a wood stove. Whoever arrived first built the fire.

Few people attended Sunday school, but the house was full for worship service. The pastor, Brother Moon, was from a nearby community and traveled by horseback to get there. He would always arrive early enough on Saturday evening for conference and worship service, spend the night with one of the members and after church services and dinner the next day would start for home. About the only times Bro Moon's family was able to come with him was during the revivals. The services were held nightly and in the daytime also. They usually lasted for at least two weeks and the building would not hold all the people. People sat around the edge of the pulpit and anywhere else they could find a seat. Some stood outside the windows looking in. The children were well behaved. The mothers with small children sat on the two seats close to the back door so if they had to leave, they could be discreet.

After many years, sitting on the rail seats, the church decided it was time to get new pews. Funds for the project were acquired in various ways. Early one Saturday morning my father and uncle started out in a wagon, pulled by a team of horses. They visited all the homes in the community, asking for hens to sell, with the proceeds going to help pay for the new church benches. They soon gathered up about 35 to 40 hens, selling them to the local produce market in Rocky Hill for one dollar each. The benches cost around two hundred dollars in all.

Meanwhile the ladies were not idle. Each one made a block to be put together into a quilt. Each block had names embroidered on them. In order to have your name included on the quilt, you had to pay a ten cent fee. After all the blocks were sewn together into an attractive pink and while quilt top, it was sold at auction to the highest bidder by a local auctioneer, Mr. Pate Hagan. The event took place in front of the Rocky Hill grocery store owned by Mr. Earl Wheeler. It was purchased by my father, Jeff Crump, for eight dollars. I can remember sleeping under it on countless nights and reading the names. Now, I wish we had not slept under it so much so it would be in better condition. I found it in the attic at my mothers the other day and it is definitely well worn. We, again, had fun reading all the names and sharing memories about the people they belonged to. I remembered many of them myself and was reminded that my mother probably remembered more of them than anyone else since she is most likely the oldest in the community.

The church acquired its first piano in July, 1946 and in June, 1950, voted to have full time services. One year later, the congregation voted to go back to only half time. That same year an extensive remodeling of the building began. The walls were covered with a pretty, light pink and purple striped, suede-looking material and the ceiling was white. All the woodwork was painted white and the stones for the foundation were replaced with solid concrete block underpinning. White asbestos shingles were used to cover the outside.

The original building underwent many changes and improvements. In September, 1967, the church voted to construct a new building in the near future and started a building fund. It was not until April, 1976, that the construction actually began and was soon finished. The replacement was a much larger, beautiful new brick building that sat in the same place as the other one.

(Most of this information was taken from the 'History of PORTLAND ASSOCIATION of GENERAL BAPTIST 1921-1979, contributed by Nora Buttram)

In the years since my family attended Fairview General Baptist Church the people have added on to the building, made many improvements and included a baptistery. It is a wonderful landmark as well as 'a lighthouse on a hill' for the community. The light in the steeple lights it up at night and in the autumn, especially when the leaves are crimson, it is a lovely country picture.

Today, it stands as a beacon in the community. When I go there I am almost like a stranger. Few of the people who attended when I did are still there. I miss them but am delighted to see many people from the community taking part and assuming the responsibility to carry on the work of God's Kingdom on earth. It pleases me that what I was once a part of in one place, I am still a part of in another. The Kingdom of God is like that. It has no end.

I have included this history of my home church where I grew up because I feel one cannot stress too much the importance that the family plays in the life of a child. I am so grateful for my ancestral history and wish I knew it all the way back to Christ. I do know that both my maternal grandfathers were preachers and my paternal grandparents were church attendees also.

FAMILY IS MONUMENTAL

The influence of family is so strong that it should be handled as carefully as any explosive or drug. What we teach and expose our children to when they are growing up will either be a great asset or a huge stumbling block in their adult life. When my children were small I was so young myself that I don't think I fully realized the extent of this truth. My husband and I did the best we knew and that was what we had been taught by our parents. Most of it was a positive in our case but if it had been a negative it would have been the same. This is another primary reason I am so grateful for my heritage.

Most of us think pretty highly of ourselves, especially when we are young, and believe we turned out alright so that is what we teach our children. I'm afraid many times people don't even think about it, they just do it by instinct. This is not necessarily a good thing. I think of a young friend of mine marrying a guy whose father had abandoned his mother and her children when he was young. He vehemently declared that he would never do such a thing to his children, but, in a few short years, he did. I have seen children imitate their parents in so many ways it is scary.

Even though my husband and I learned more as we experienced life and became older it was too late to use that wisdom in raising our boys because they were already young adults. It was only after they were in college that I recognized that our example was more influential than our words. I noticed how much of our thinking and actions were instilled in them by reading the themes they wrote for school and watching their mannerisms in conversation with others. I wish someone had told me, "Watch very carefully what you do and say. You are teaching your children to be that way!"

Another frustrating thing about the situation is that it is too late to break the cycle. We have already taught our children and that is what they will teach their children if something drastic doesn't change it. As a grandparent I have tried hard to point this out to our children but another truth I have learned is that when children have become adults they are past the ideal teaching stage for parents, and I suppose that is as it should be. This is just another good reason to be aware of how really important those parenting years are.

I have heard my mother say that there were many things she wished she had done differently when raising her children but at the time she did not know how important it was. She said she always prayed that God would 'take up the slack' and make up for the things she did not know or was incapable of doing. I think He answered that prayer pretty well so I am following her example. Again! I do believe that God knows our heart's desire because in Psalms 37: 4 it says, *"Delight yourself in the Lord and He will give you the desire of your heart."* To me, it means the same thing as Matthew 6:33. (*"Seek ye first the kingdom of God and His righteousness and all of these things shall be added."*)

The church family is hopefully an extension of the nuclear family, especially when it is a smaller church such as ours was. One of the negative aspects of belonging to a small church is also one of the pluses. Everyone becomes family and that is a very good thing, especially in the impersonal world of today, but, if and when you should have to leave, it is very difficult. Just because something is difficult is no reason not to do it. It is, in fact, probably more reason to see it through. Any kind of change in our lives that takes us out of our comfort zone is going to take effort but most of the time the effort is more than worth the price. Personal growth usually comes about by way of pain, embarrassment, education, effort and a dozen other means, but it must come. Otherwise we will grow stagnant in our spiritual lives and become good for nothing as it says in comparing us to salt in Matthew 5:13.

Sounds of Time
The covers were heavy
When winter winds blew cold,
Snug between two sisters
Heated by our bodies mold.

The first sounds of morning,
Daddy stoking the old stove
Grating ashes for new breath
Watching crackling flames unfold.

Mama's in the kitchen,
Breakfast is in the making,
I hear her cheerful whistling
And smell the biscuits baking!

The years fly like an eagle,
The house grows silently still
Another generation is launched
Like grass growing on a hill;

Memories of sounds past
Play melodies in my mind
I hear them sharp and clear
As the scrolls of time unwind;

Mama humming gospel songs
Daddy singing them by note,
Sister playing the piano
From tunes that others wrote.

"Amazing Grace,"
How sweet the sounds
I hear from days gone by
They shall forever be to me
Like angels from on high.

CHANGES ARE STEPPING STONES

We moved to Warren County in 1979 and live near the town of Smiths Grove, Kentucky. I always felt that a person should be able to go to any church that believes in worshipping the one true God. It did not make sense to me to travel a far distance to attend church services when there are churches nearby. We slowly began to attend the Baptist Church in Smiths Grove on certain occasions and continued to go back to Fairview where we were members. After a period of time we decided to change our membership to Smiths Grove Baptist Church. It was my husband that strongly encouraged the issue and I agreed with his decision but it was harder for me to leave my home church than I thought it would be. Since it was a small church and mostly family, I wrote a letter to the clerk expressing why we had made the decision to leave. I did not want anyone to think we were leaving for any negative reasons as so often seems to be the case. It is a sad thing, to me, for Christians to not be able to get along with other Christians to the point of having to leave a membership because of disagreement. I repeat what I said earlier, "If anyone should be able to get along with each other is should be Christians." On the other hand, I realize that God works in mysterious ways and many times His work flourishes and grows by new churches being started because of a split in a congregation – but we should still be able to do it agreeably.

The Bible, our guide, says that God's instructions to us hinge on two commands. The first is 'to love the Lord our God with all of our heart, soul and strength, and the second is to love our neighbor as ourselves.' That's a pretty big order but surely it is necessary since it is mentioned several times in the scriptures. I realize that we are humans, as a lot of people like to say to excuse themselves of their shortcomings, but I believe the desire must be in our hearts and the effort will follow. The Bible is explicit in telling us that we can not be saved by good works (Eph. 2:9) but it also tells us in James 2:20 that faith without works is dead. I believe this is talking about good works done physically, with your hands, mind and body.

These two important commands have to do with our life in the spiritual realm. Things of the spirit are not things that can be experienced by our five senses. However, our physical senses certainly can assist us in understanding and enjoying the spiritual realm. Love is a spiritual entity. You can not see it, touch it, feel it with your hand, smell it or taste it. This does not mean it is any less important. All of the things that make life meaningful are controlled by our spirit. Desires, attitudes, thoughts, relationships, passions, feelings, moods, and motivations are a few good examples. Entities of the spirit can be good or bad, depending on the source. As Christians we believe bad spirits are from the devil, or Satan, who is the prince of the physical world and the father of all lies. In John 10:10, Jesus says he (Satan) came to kill, steal and destroy life and all that is good and he does this through our spirit. (Matthew 16:22, Luke 22:3 and Acts 4:3 are examples of his work and Isaiah 14: 12-24 is the history of how he came to be.) Some of the by-products of the spirit of Satan are listed in Galatians 5:19-21. They include adultery, fornication, uncleanness, lasciviousness, idolatry, witchcraft, hatred, variance, emulations, wrath, strife, seditions, heresies, envyings, murders, drunkenness, revellings and such things. (This list is from the King James Version. If you want definitions I suggest you look this scripture up in the Living Bible or The New International Version.) The scripture goes on to say that those who do these things shall not inherit the Kingdom of God.

On the other hand the bi-products of the Holy Spirit (the Bible calls them fruits) are listed in the next two verses: namely, love, joy, peace, longsuffering, gentleness, goodness, faith, meekness, and temperance. It would be wonderful if all Christians produced such fruit from their lives and many do. We all can if we allow the Holy Spirit to be in charge of our thinking on a continuous basis. I am not saying this is easy, only possible. The thing we cannot do for sure is live righteously without the help of the Holy Spirit. Paul, spiritual giant that he was, said in Romans 7:14-25, it is impossible without Jesus Christ our Lord doing it for us.

I took an evangelism class one time and at the end of the course the teacher's only assignment was for each student to write a paper describing the perfect church. My paper was written based on a church that actively exhibited and practiced these nine fruits of the spirit listed in Galatians. The following is what I wrote. What do you think?

(Keep in mind that this is only a description of an imaginary church, not a real one.)

(THE PERFECT CHURCH)

A light, a city on a hill, salt . . . all are symbolic of the perfect church.

The 'city on a hill' represents Jerusalem that was built on a high hill and was where the Israelites, God's chosen people in the Old Testament, came to meet with Him in worship and get instruction for how to live.

The light represents Jesus who is called the Light of the

World. He provides guidance and power to bring us out of the darkness of sin and into the light of His love. This light provides power to illuminate our minds and act as a guiding beacon to us; in turn, our lights shine, providing illumination to others.

Salt provides flavor; it is a necessary ingredient in our diet and a way of preservation. I believe the Church (all Christians) offer the same essentials to our world.

Jesus said in Matthew 5: 13-17 (NIV) *"You are the salt of the earth. But if the salt loses its saltiness, how can it be made salty again? It is no longer good for anything, except to be thrown out and trampled by men.*

You are the light of the world. A city on a hill cannot be hidden. Neither do people light a lamp and put it under a bowl. Instead they put it on its stand, and it gives light to everyone in the house. In the same way, let your light shine before men, that they may see your good deeds and praise your Father in heaven."

Jesus was teaching his disciples these things because He had chosen them to establish His church (kingdom) on earth. As the church was in the beginning, so it should be today.

The church is also a family and every part is equally important, although they serve many different functions. There are many brothers and sisters in the family and they all love and support one another. Of course they don't always agree on the minor details of life (how boring it would be if they did), but they respect one another enough to trust them to work out their own salvation. I think this can be true because we all have the same father and the kinship of the Holy Spirit keeps love in control regardless of our individual likes and dislikes.

Even though we have different cultures, habits, time schedules, vocations and a variety of other things, still there are many things all Christians should embody.

Basically, these are things that are not visible to the human eye but are seen by people more quickly and keenly than one can imagine. The bible lists them in Galatians 5:22&23 and refers to them as the 'fruits of the Spirit.'

Remember, fruit is the natural response of a good healthy seed.

I will attempt to list them individually and not necessarily in order of importance.

LOVE seems to be the governing agent that shines forth from each personality. I'm not talking about the kind that one has for a friend who returns it or the romantic kind that seems to take away our good sense. The love I'm speaking of is amazing in that it expects nothing in return, omits no one, even works with overt enemies, and seems to be the automatic response no matter what the situation. This love expresses a spirit of kindness, patience and selflessness that melts away anger, envy, selfishness, rudeness, pride and a plethora of other evil spirits that bring so much pain and disaster to human relationships.

A one word description would be "unconditional." The origin of this kind of love comes from God who first showed it to us by His Son, Jesus. Once we have received this type of love we are then, and only then, capable of extending it to others.

If my perfect church has a creed to live by and center their actions toward, it would be "Love the Lord our God with all your heart, mind and body, and love everyone else like you love yourself."

The references we are given are the sixty-six books of the Bible which contain many examples of real-life situations, wisdom of the ages, admonitions to guide us, prophesies fulfilled and the words of Jesus that teach us what we must do in order to be empowered with this kind of love. The importation comes through the Holy Spirit which is imparted to us and lives in us when we are born of the Spirit. What a dynamic thing it is to possess and use for the glory of God. This love and care we show for one another amazes people who are not Christians because it is so uncommon in the secular world. The Book of I John is a wonderful resource for helping one understand more fully this kind of love. Among other things, it tells us that people will know we are Christians by the way we love each other and if we don't we are none of His.

SELF CONTROL is another attribute that is exhibited by the members of this church. There are no written covenants, or agreements to be adhered to except God's word. The Laws of Moses were given to show the people of God how far off they were from being the people God desired. Jesus told us the laws were to be written in our hearts which means when we keep Jesus' way the priority of our life, and motivation of our heart, we will do what pleases God because we love him and not because we feel we have to. When any member of the church fails to do what is best for them and their relationship with God, the other members will do everything within their power to encourage and assist them in making things right again. Sometimes one might really have a struggle in changing old habits which do not bring glory to God and we are to be very patient and loving toward them. We know there is a possibility that it might be us the next time . . . .there, but for the grace of God, go I!

Anger, impatience, jealousy, hatred, negative thoughts, envy, lust, immorality, manipulation, bribery, etc. are displeasing to God because they come from the heart and are of the spirit. Jesus said these are the things we, as Christians, must have control over. If we concentrate on ridding our hearts of them, the outward actions will follow suit. We need to teach new converts, and each other, to nurture our relationship with God daily and walk in the Spirit so as to allow him to monitor the control factor in our lives. Sins such as these bind our spirit and keep us from being productive in our personal lives, in society and certainly in the kingdom of God.

PEACE is something a lot of people talk about and say they want but few seem to have. The ones who have mastered the art of letting go and accepting the direction of the flow of the Holy Spirit that comes their way demonstrate a calmness of soul that is very attractive. It shows on the face, in the way we walk, our body gestures, our voice, our speech, our health and is reflected from the soul through our eyes. We don't worry, fret, get upset about minor things and reserve the major ones for righteous indignation against an idea not a person. We remember that we wrestle not against flesh and blood but against principalities and powers of the evils of Satan and his demons.

Knowing that flesh cannot fight with spirit, we allow the Holy Spirit to win the battle His way. We just submit our human resources to him, and victory is sure.

JOY is pleasure that takes the place of the happiness a majority of people are seeking. Happiness is exciting, but fleeting, and often has the opposite of depression as its pursuer. To be fulfilled is more important than to be ecstatically happy. Joy is continuous, rewarding and restful to the mind and spirit. It puts a smile in the heart as well as on the lips and in the eyes. This smile is evidence of God in our heart and a compelling witness to the unsaved world. Circumstances around us can be in chaos but it is possible to still have the joy of our salvation within.

PATIENCE is scarce in our society today. If it could be manufactured, bottled and put on the market for sale, what a money-making commodity it would be. Millions of people are in a tremendous hurry to get somewhere or do something so they can go somewhere else and do something else. They spend so much time in planning and anticipating the future, they miss the present. In the perfect church we have learned to live in the present. We are convinced that not many things are a matter of life or death, nor worth 'getting our panties in a wad' about. . . . as Troy Richards used to say. Practicing patience makes life pleasant for ourselves and those around us and is easier on our health as well.

KINDNESS AND GENTLENESS are gifts that are never wasted and more appreciated than silver or gold. A hand on the shoulder, a pat on the back, an encouraging word, a well-timed compliment, a hearty handshake, a genuine smile, and monetary generosity are common, everyday occurrences among our members. These things are not only extended to each other but to all they interact with at home, at work and play.

GOODNESS is a word that describes the overall nature of our people but it is not something they exhibit intentionally. If someone told them they were good, they would be quick to say, "Not me, it is only the spirit of God within me," and that would be true. Even Jesus said, *"There is none good but the Father in heaven."* (Luke 18:19)

FAITHFULNESS is the thread that holds us all together in love and harmony. Not faithfulness to a doctrine, creed, or each other, but to God who is the maker and creator of us all. His spirit is what unites us as one and makes us able to recognize our Christian brothers and sisters wherever we meet them.

The physical aspects of our worship and service to God and others are not very complicated. Our building is an old one and in a small town. It is of unique structure and is appreciated for its' history. This could be a problem, but does not have to be. When we keep our priorities right, these small details are not important. To be a good steward of the peoples' offerings, we believe we should make the best possible use of our facilities. The auditorium has beautiful stained glass windows from the late eighteen hundreds. It adds to the reverence and holiness of the place and we love it. It can not only be used for worship for the congregation but for a comforting solace when an individual needs a place to get away from the stresses of life and refresh, renew and restore their soul. It is a perfect place for weddings and family occasions.

The beautiful windows and reverence of the place do not keep it from being a comfortable and inviting place to everyone who enters, despite their origin, nationality, cultural practices, monetary status, social status or creed. Dress ranges from formal to very informal. The exterior is not nearly as important as the inner man and that is what we are concerned with. Our worship style ranges from hand-clapping choruses to moving ethereal hymns. To make the best use of our auditorium, we have two worship services on Sunday and Bible study in between. People choose when they want to come and if there is not room when they come they just go to the Methodist church or the Christian church which is one block away and are happy to do so. We have six church buildings in the small town of 1000 people and anyone is welcome in any of them even though they are different denominations.

Our classroom facilities are adequate and comfortable and our nursery is spacious, clean and has wonderful men and women who serve there. The kitchen and dining area is inviting, clean and cheerfully decorated. The meals we enjoy together are celebrations and everyone feels welcome. Any group is free to use it when available and always leaves it clean and ready for the next event. Our people are wonderful cooks and love to use their gift of hospitality in creating good foods to share with others. We have a Christian bar in town that is shared by all the churches where people who are lonesome or just want company for an evening can go and grab a sandwich, play a game with someone or just visit. Everyone feels welcome and it is a very busy place. There is music and respectable dancing; a good place to let your hair down, relax, have some fun and exercise our childlike qualities.

We have considered having play-school for our children and a retirement home for our aged, but, for the present, have decided that we could be better witnesses if we permeate the secular ones and share God's love and spirit in those places. We encourage our members to interact with all people so we can introduce Jesus to as many as possible. We believe knowing Jesus will make an impact on their lives, our society, and in return, on our own families. The globe has become so much smaller with advanced communications and transportation that what one of us does, ultimately affects all of us. Still yet, the great God that unites us all in one spirit is in control. Bless His Holy Name!!

Our present congregation is a group of people on many different levels of spiritual maturity. Because of this, the vision for us is varied as well. We must get out of the "I" mode in order for this to change. When we are born of the spirit of God, this is what happens. We allow our carnal bodies to be nailed to the cross and allow the resurrected Jesus to fill us with himself in the form of the Holy Spirit. This spirit unites all believers in vision and purpose and is not just recommended, but essential, for evangelism to happen.

Perhaps many in our congregation have believed in their minds and hearts but have been 'stiffed-necked' and resisted the Holy Spirit. This reminds me of the people spoken of by Stephen just before he was stoned to death. Consequently, we need a leader who is called by God, and convinced that the Book of Acts is true and can happen today as surely as it did in the first church. This belief will result in it being demonstrated in his or her life and proclaimed from the pulpit in power and might. We need to be told the story of Stephen, Ananias and Sapphira, Paul, Peter, Phillip and all the other biblical characters whose lives were changed drastically by the Holy Spirit. We need to be reminded of the miracles that took place and led to believe that by faith in the same God, miracles can still take place today. Lives can be redeemed and families, communities, and nations can be reclaimed through that power working in the lives of Christians.

Until we are convinced of this, we are just playing church and being no better than the Pharisees whom Jesus often condemned.

Once we are certain of this, we need to commit to prayer without ceasing until we are moved by the Holy Spirit to be excited about what Jesus is doing in our lives and can do in the lives of others. As He guided Paul, Silas, Barnabas, Phillip and others in their evangelism, so will He work in our church the same way and it will be effective.

As the church reaches out, people are converted and the congregation grows, changes will need to be made in the different aspects of the work. This will not be a problem if we continue using the book of Acts as our guide by choosing people who are led by the Spirit to direct our activities, both physical and spiritual.

In my opinion, we can begin all kinds of programs and have many committees but unless they are initiated by God working thru the Spirit in people's lives, they will come to naught. When He begins a work, the people who are gifted in that area will volunteer to become involved and there will be no opposition from other Christians. The only opposition will be from the evil one and he has already been defeated by Jesus

The different facets of worship, counseling, teaching, ministering to the sick, visiting the elderly who are homebound, and benevolent activities should be governed by special ministers who are chosen as a result of much prayer. They will be capable of choosing and encouraging the people who will join them in that part of the church ministry. It is important to allow people to use their gifts in the area they enjoy because the process and the results are more rewarding. Since every part of the church body is just as important as another, there is no friction about where and how we will serve, and everyone will want to serve somewhere, therefore, no one will experience burnout from duplicating areas of service.

The overall management and care of the buildings, records, finances and other physical needs should be controlled by a board of directors that is responsible for choosing specialized leaders over smaller groups or committees to be in charge of specific things. These should be men and women of integrity, wisdom, spiritual maturity, humility and holiness, with the heart of a servant.

When a problem or disagreement arises, it should be taken to the minister of whatever department it concerns, and be discussed openly and honestly in a godly matter and then prayed about until a solution is reached. Everyone does not have to agree about everything but everyone does have to love one another and allow them to disagree if it is necessary.

The thing that should be most amazing about our church to the unsaved world is 'how we love one another' and it will also be our best tool of evangelism if we will love them the same way.

Now that I have described a 'perfect' church, I will have to admit that there is surely no such thing, and probably never will be, but it gives us a goal to strive for. One of my professors in high school often quoted, "Hitch your wagon to a star." He said to make it so high that we would never reach it but it would give us something to work toward. He was also the one who said, "There are three words for achieving success. The first is 'work', the second is 'work' and the third is 'work'. He had lived thru the depression and the philosophy then was very different than today, but we would do well to take heed a little more to the teachings of that era.

TRUE LOVE

Somewhere in my past I learned that there are three different Latin words for love. **Eros** is the romantic love that makes our heart turn flip-flops, our mind go awry and puts extra light in our eyes and yet blinds them. It is the kind of love God created so that we would want to marry someone who thinks exactly opposite than we do and have children by them that will give us more heartaches than we ever dreamed of having. Of course the pleasures and rewards of marriage and child bearing are great also, but I wonder how many of us would choose to marry and have children if we knew how difficult it was going to be. I have often thought that God just pulled a slick one on us but I'm sure He knew what He was doing. I really do believe that He had our welfare in mind when He determined that we would not be able to know the future.

Thru the years I have often contemplated why God made men and women entirely different and then attracted us so strongly to each other. I believe it was part of the curse He put on Adam and Eve for their sin in the Garden of Eden. (Gen. 3:16-19) Woman's desire would always be for a man even if he did rule over her and man would desire a woman to love and provide and protect even though he had to work hard and face many difficulties in understanding and relating to her. Many times the attraction is not only to the opposite sex but to one with the opposite personality as well. I finally came to see that all of this is for our benefit. When we marry someone who thinks very differently from us, each one must be willing to give up much of their way in order to get along and enjoy the results that they both desire. Sometimes one or the other, or both, mistakenly think that having children will help their relationship. It changes their relationship but does not necessarily solve any problems. It only requires that both of us give up even more of ourselves for the little one who has arrived and depends on us. This giving up of ourselves in both instances is not easy but is very good for us. God is possibly advancing us on the pathway that will eventually lead and enable us to give up our way to His way. The more I learn, the more I am amazed that He knew all along what He was doing. Through it all He is trying to teach us to trust Him. If we knew the future we might never take the leap and invite the pain that has to come with our learning. Now that I am older and have passed through the worst hurdles (I hope) I can truthfully say I would do it again but maybe give myself a chance to be wiser when I took the leap. I don't know if that is possible or not.

Eros love comes from inside a person's heart and mind and is of the spirit but it is very much affected and controlled by physical things. The enjoyment of a relationship of this kind of love is enhanced by being able to see, hear, touch, taste and feel the loved one. Because of this there is a danger of allowing Satan to deceive us by convincing us that the fleshly things are more important than fruits of the Holy Spirit in maintaining a good eros relationship. It is not true. If we are not careful he will deceive us as he did Adam and Eve.

Another kind of love is referred to as **phileo** love which is a brotherly kind of love. This is the kind of love we have for our family and close friends; the kind that is returned to us in like manner. To remember it, think of the city of Philadelphia which is known as the 'city of brotherly love'.

The kind of love that we should have for God and all people is called **agape** love. The 13th chapter of I Corinthians gives a good explanation of what this kind of love includes. It is a much higher and more encompassing type that can only be possessed by people who have the Holy Spirit living in them. The Holy Spirit is the one who loves with agape love through the individual.

This love is unconditional and belongs to a category all its' own. It is not human to love unconditionally. A mother's love is extremely strong and can withstand a multitude of trials but we know and hear of many instances where mothers kill their children or abuse them. Given the right circumstances we humans are capable of very inhumane things. This definitely is not God's plan for his creation. That is the reason He provided a way for us to escape getting to the place where we could do such a thing. Jesus came to earth as a human, just like us, to set the example for how we could live in harmony with Him and each other as we were created to do. Some of you will say that he was human but he was also divine and we are not. That is true, but he used his power of divinity only in developing the way for us to have access to that same divinity. All the miracles he performed were to show us how much power we can have access to, in and through him. His purpose was to establish the Kingdom of God on earth while He was present in human flesh so that we could continue it after He had gone back to the Father. He knew we would be too weak in our own capabilities to carry on this work especially since we have to contend with Satan. Satan is a spirit and the only thing that can defeat him is another spirit. The spiritual world is separate from the physical world, thus, Satan has to be fought on his own turf. This is the reason He sent the Holy Spirit to be available in any place, at any time, to aid us when we need and request His help. Our problem

SING UNTO THE LORD!

Singing praises to God is one of the oldest and best ways to worship Him. You may say, "I cannot sing" but he hears the heart song more than the audible one from our lips. He is pleased no matter how it sounds when it is to honor Him. I remember asking an uncle one time why he never sang at church. He said he sang only while he was driving the tractor so no one could hear him. The tractor motor drowned out the noise but he still received the joy from doing it . . . and if it was to God, I'm sure He heard and loved it.

The Bible says *"Make a joyful noise unto the Lord, Serve the Lord with gladness, come before His presence with Thanksgiving."* Psalm 100: 1&2 (KJV) God sees into our heart as if thru a magnifying glass and has no problem determining if we are thinking about what we are singing or if we are just mouthing the words. If one is concentrating too hard on making sure every note is just exactly right it is impossible to have one's spirit and mind on worship. He also knows if we are singing it for His glory or for our own.

That is not to say that trained voices cannot worship God. They can, without a doubt; we just have to make sure it is to honor Him and not ourselves. I'm sure other people get more enjoyment from hearing it but to God it all sounds the same. Probably a good question to ask would be, "When people hear it, do they give praise to God for creating such talent in an individual or do they praise the individual?" When it is sincerely from the heart He is surely pleased and glorified with great anthems and flawlessly sung renditions of all types of musical selections that rise and fall with the notes in perfect harmony making the music flow like Niagara Falls or a trickling brook. Such music lifts the spirit and grips the heart and squeezes it until it hurts so bad that tears come through our eyes and flow down our cheeks.

I heard someone say one time, "If the eyes leek, the head doesn't swell."

Isn't that what true worship is all about?

It may be that some songs of praise should only be sung in private between an individual and God. If this is the case, and it is not known by the singer, then the listener should be patient and remember that God is more pleased with imperfect, but genuine praise, than He is with a critical heart.

I have never had a good singing voice but that has not kept me from singing, in church . . . probably to a lot of peoples' dismay . . . and when alone.

Whichever way we experience music, if it connects us with the Creator of the universe and lifts our mind and spirit above our earthly, everyday thinking, it is called 'worship.' Both the deliverer and the hearer are responsible for the conditions of their own mind and heart that will determine if this happens for them. For this reason, the same worship service can be very helpful to one person and not at all beneficial to another.

Recently I went back to the church where I grew up. It was enormously satisfying to sing along with the congregation the old songs I had sung there many years ago. I did not even need to read the words because they were still in my memory. My voice is not trained and neither is anyone else's that attends there but my participation resulted in true worship. My spirit was moved and lifted by the words that I considered as I sang them.

One of the reasons I noticed this was probably

because at the church where we presently go the worship teams rarely ever sing the same songs enough for me to memorize them. I would never admit that it might be because I am quite a bit older now and my ability to retain them is diminished!

The words are projected on a large screen where I can read them, and that helps, but it is still hard to read unfamiliar lyrics, sing along with an unknown tune and be able to apply them to my mind and heart at the same time. I usually do sing along, but not with gusto, because of this reason. However, as with most situations, one advantage to joining in with worship here is that it is so loud your voice cannot be heard by others and it is not embarrassing to sing out if you wish to, even if you are not a good singer. It is kind of like singing into the wind while driving a tractor and plowing a field!

With the current generation there has been much controversy in many churches about the kind of music that should be used and the type of songs to be sung. Perhaps some kind of controversy has always been prevalent in moving from one generation to another but this is my era and the one I am familiar with.

People my age and older usually love the old hymns accompanied by organ and/or piano music. The younger generations prefer a mixture of many musical instruments. Stringed instruments, percussion and brass are sometimes used with the piano.

'Praise songs' is the term they use for their worship songs of choice. They are usually short verses that repeat themselves and are frequently projected onto a screen while the congregation follows along singing. The words are often taken from scripture and I think that is a good thing. Many are newly composed by members of the worship teams from their personal experiences. They are often very meaningful.

Younger people complain that all of the old songs talk about going to heaven and how wonderful it will be and they are not as much interested in that as they are in the here and now. This is understandable but a little extreme. Many traditional songs do speak of the hereafter but certainly not the highest percentage. Many of the hymns were written by godly people who walked and communed with God and were inspired to write down their thoughts which were put to music. Many times inspiration does come from extreme emotions caused by pain and suffering or even great happiness. I believe this is also true of many of the newer 'praise songs' that are written today.

I love them both and really see no conflict. The conflict comes, I believe, when someone wants to be in control of how things are done in their church. One solution that many churches have tried is to have a mixture of both kinds. This works only if the congregation is large enough and financially able to make it happen. Surely God is not pleased when His people create conflict over what kinds of songs they are going to sing in worshipping Him.

Somehow that seems to me to be a little absurd?

What is worship all abou anyway? In my mind, I think it is something like this.

Today Was A Good Day

Today was a good day, I made a new friend
And talked to old ones--
Today was a good day,
I read an inspiring and interesting book,
That stabbed my heart to tears.
Today was a good day,
I listened to great music that lifted my spirit high
And was moved to sing a song--

Today was a good day, I was hugged by someone
Who loves me very much.
Today was a good day, I learned a new word
For my old vocabulary.
Today was a good day, I cooked good food
For people that I love--
Today was a good day, I suffered physical pain,
And was reminded of how thankful I am
For a good healthy body--
Today was a good day, I worshiped my Lord
Who made my day good!

My Praise

Blue skies
White fluffy clouds
Green leaves
Turning lovely colors
In dying
May we as your
Children
Do the same.

Thanks
For fresh air
Urging us on
To breathe deeply
Of your love
Your spirit
Increasing our
Gratefulness

What beauty

All of nature
What miracles
Our bodies
How marvelous
Sight, sound, touch
Taste and smell.

How glorious
Our pilgrimage
In this world
Not just exist
But experience
Your world
Your love
You!

The Bible has a lot of praises to God and singing in it. Singing praises is at its best when it cannot be held back. The spirit within is so full and grateful it overflows and bursts into song. I think of Moses and all the Israelites exuberantly praising and thanking God by bursting into the song we find in Exodus, chapter 15. God had just parted the waters of the Red Sea and the Israelites had crossed over onto dry land. The Israelites had then witnessed their enemy, the Egyptians, drowned by the waters as they rolled back at exactly the right time. Certainly they had something to sing about. It says Miriam, Moses and Aaron's sister who was a prophetess, was so excited she led the other women in dancing while shaking timbrels in their hands to the beat of the music.

Another song that overflowed from the spirit within was the one Mary, the mother of Jesus, sang when she went to visit her cousin, Elizabeth. The minute Mary saw her, Elizabeth acknowledged she already knew about her good news. I'm sure it must have been gratifying to Mary for Elizabeth to confirm the miracle inside her body and share her own belief and knowledge that it was indeed the son of God. (Luke 1:46-55) Mary's song is a beautiful tribute to God for all He had already done and was about to do.

The book of Psalms is full of praises that were mostly written by King David when he was a young man. I can see him now, sitting in the shade of a rock, watching over the sheep and composing songs with his harp, and whatever other musical instruments he played. He must have been like my uncle who sang as loud as he wanted to because there was no one there to hear him. I don't believe he had any idea of those songs being recorded in a book that would be passed down for the next two hundred centuries and sang by people who worship the same God he did. I think he must have just written them from an intimate relationship and a heart overflowing with love for a God that could create all the marvelous things of nature that he could see around him.

I do not keep sheep but often I do retreat to the woods to refresh my spirit and be reminded of the omnipotence of the God I love and serve and who loves me. As far as I am concerned one of the best ways that the government spends our money is using it to preserve and protect our national and state parks. Man is very smart and can design and build many beautiful and creative things but, in my opinion, nature's beauties cannot be surpassed. There is something about it that inspires the soul and refreshes the spirit. If that inspiration is strong enough, one just might break into song!

The following poems were written while seeking refuge in the woods at Mammoth Cave National Park near where I live.

Alone With God

Silence,
A crow call,
Faint, faraway voices,
But, I am alone.

A leaf falls
To the earth beneath;
Making no sound,
Ah, grace and peace.

Magnificent rocks,
Boulders of stone,
Create a ridge
How, unknown!

Quiet! Stillness!
I'm listening;
Speak, God,
From your throne--

A doe approaches,
Another one appears,
Separated by the ridge,
Formed thru the years--

The little one seeks
For a way across,
Finally enough courage,
To risk the loss;

Runs fast to the other,
He's found his mother!
He vigorously attempts
To nurse her milk
Only a little,

She walks away,
They roam around,
I watch them slowly
Enjoy their day!

Not a hint of breeze
Through the trees
Only the rattle
Of colorful leaves;

I look around,
A gray squirrel peeks
Around the tree;
Wondering if he,
Can trust such as me

Away down below
A river flows,
Where the end is,
I do not know.

The deer watch me,
Pondering if,
I am a threat
To their world--

Silently I sit
Among the trees,
Still as they
As if to freeze!

They wander away,
Now out of sight,
It won't be long
Until the night--

I hear the whistle
From far away,
The tourist boat
On mission today--

Listening, I hear
Birds giving forth
The songs of flight
On wings so light,
It all seems right!

Their gift to God
And mortals below
If only I could stay,
But I must go
Back to work
To help others see
The worth of nature
To you and me--

To become as one,
For only a while,
Removes the stress
And brings a smile--

My eyes cannot see
An end anywhere,
To the woods
That gave me
A blessing so rare--

It must have been
God's beautiful plan
To provide such care
For mortal man--

Help me remember
The time I spent
Alone with God
And what it meant!

Autumn By The River

The River is silent,
Stillness like death;
Over eons of time
It has drifted by
Right past this spot
Among the trees
Taking their place
Standing straight and tall
Waiting for each autumn
To show their radiance
And then give it up
To the good earth

How rich it must be
From ages of leaves
Dropped on schedule
Year after year

The colors of autumn
Challenge my eyes
To remember when
Their gaze has met
More golden hues
With God's true greens

Blended in symmetry

I set my glance
On far away hills
And ponder the distance
By animal path

Tree voices speak
Thru soft breezes
Making harmony
In musical sounds
Over the valleys,
Down to the river,
And into forever

To feel God touch
My spirit and soul
Thru His creation
From ages of old
Is life renewing
Like morn at dawn
Or setting of sun
No matter the time
His work is done.

I am grateful for the many lyrics and tunes of songs I still know today that I learned in Sunday school and church as a little girl. A few days ago I was at my piano, playing songs from the book that was used in my childhood church. Like riding a bicycle, the words and music came back instantly.

Even though I do not sing a lot today, I am frequently reminded of the lines of a song as I go about my daily routine of life.

Our memory bank is filled when we are young and our mind can absorb things like a sponge. The older we get the harder it is to retain information. We understand and remember it for a short time but we can recall the ones from early in our lives better. Please be reminded that this is one important reason to take your children to church when they are small. You will be surprised how much they will get from the service that you are unaware of. Nurseries are nice for stressed out parents, and when your children are very small, but don't wait too long to let them sit in the pew with the family. They may wiggle and squirm a bit but they will learn soon enough if you are firm and persistent with them. Believe me, they are smarter at a younger age than you may think and it is very good for them to learn about God and how to worship Him.

Good nurseries will have teachers, not just caretakers. Minds are a valuable thing and should not be wasted. Churches should use the one or two hours available to teach them about Jesus and the scriptures. For some, it may be the only kind of bible teaching they experience. Seeds sown in fertile soil will sprout and grow sooner or later. We need to make sure they are good seed.

WHY PRAY?

I believe it would be difficult to worship God without praying. After all, to love and adore someone creates an automatic desire to let that someone know about it. In fact, it is almost impossible not to shout it from the mountain tops if you have the opportunity.

Love demands a response from the giver as well as the receiver.

I believe it is fitting to compare our relationship with God to our earthly relationships in order to gain a better understanding of them. If you have a family member or a good friend that is very important to you, would you not want to spend time with that person often? Would you not want to share the good things that happen in your life with them? When you are hurting, confused, angry, or whatever, is it not good to have someone whom you can confide in and make you feel better?

Sometimes our earthly friends can encourage, console, support and cheer us up, but many times they are as helpless to solve our problems as we are. Many times they may not understand or are not available when we need them. Sooner or later another human being, no matter how perfect we think they are, will disappoint us, not because they want to or intend to but because they are human and fallible.

These are the occasions when prayer is such a comfort. Knowing that God is always available and cares about everything we care about is heartening to the soul and spirit.

Many times people have a misconception about God and how he wants us to commune with Him. I heard my aunt say one time that she always felt she should not bother God with the little things in life because He was too busy taking care of big things. One problem with that idea is that what she thinks are the little things, God may see as the big things. It also limits God and I believe He is unlimited in power, scope, knowledge, or any other way imaginable. What a privilege to have an ever present and all knowing friend who loves us even more than we love ourselves and desires a relationship with us! It seems only a fool would not want in on such an opportunity.

Of course, I believe God does expect something from us as well. He wants sincerity and humility for one thing. He strongly condemned the Pharisees who made a big show of their rituals of praying and worshiping so everybody could see them and think them important. In fact, in Matthew 6: 5-15, Jesus gives us some straightforward advice on praying. He says to do it in secret, just between you and Him, and not to recite the same prayers over and over. Then He gave us an example to go by that has become known as "The Lord's Prayer." Many times people do repeat this prayer, and I am not going to say that is wrong but I will say when we use it we should be sure we are thinking about what the words mean and be sincere in saying them. This is true, no matter what words we use. I have heard long, written out, oratorical and liturgical prayers prayed and I have heard a few words mumbled inaudibly or barely uttered from the mouth of an untrained person. Others seem to think if they cry loud enough they can make their prayers reach heaven by sheer vocal power. I believe the important issue to God is the absence of hypocrisy which means it is sincerely from the mind and heart and in the right spirit. If it is, I believe He hears it and will answer in His time and wisdom. Don't ever mistake your time and wisdom for His. Sometimes they are as far apart as night and day. Another requirement is unquestioning faith in God's ability to perform and in complete submission to His will.

The Bible speaks of different postures a person may have while praying.

In Numbers 16:22, it says they fell upon their faces; In I Kings 8:22, Solomon stood before the Lord and spread forth his hands toward heaven; I Chronicles 21: 16, says when David saw the angel, he and the elders clothed themselves in sackcloth and fell upon their faces; In Psalms 28:2 and Lamentations 2:19, it mentions lifting up holy hands; in Psalms 95:6 it says 'let us bow down and kneel before the Lord, our maker and Luke 22:41 says Jesus kneeled down and prayed to His Father in the Garden of Gethsemane. A little while later it says in Matthew 26:39 that He fell on his face, and prayed, saying, *O my Father, if it be possible, let this cup pass from me*: nevertheless not as I will, but as thou wilt."

Again, posture should not be the object of our concern when praying. The position of the heart is what is crucial, but I will say, that may be what controls our posture at times. It does seem the more earnest the prayer and the more humble the spirit, the lower the body.

I don't believe anyone is excluded when it comes to what or whom we should pray for. The Bible is specific in pointing out we should pray for our enemies and those who despitefully use or persecute us. We need to pray for fellow Christians and for ourselves like the publican did in Luke 18:13. In Psalms 1:32 it says pray for the peace of Jerusalem and I'm sure all other nations, as well. If we don't know what to pray for, in Romans 8:26, it says the Holy Spirit will do it for us.

I believe God is pleased when we have needs and bring them to Him. He promises to answer us if the conditions are right, such as John 15:7 which says, *"If ye abide in me, and my words abide in you, ye shall ask what ye will, and it shall be done unto you."*

He is also pleased when we come to Him with a grateful heart to express our thanks for His blessings and when we just want to spend time in His presence. There is no better tonic for the soul and spirit, as well as our physical body and emotions, than to spend a few hours alone with God, talking and listening to Him. It is as refreshing to the inner body as a shower is to the outward body.

I'm glad we do not have to wait for special times such as these to touch base with Him, so to speak. Romans 12:12b says   . . 'continuing instant in prayer' and I Thessalonians 5:17 tells us to 'pray without ceasing. Jesus sits at the right hand of God, twenty four/seven, listening and waiting for us to connect with Him. If the Holy Spirit is in our heart, we have constant access to His power. I find it easy to talk to Him, sometimes audibly, as I go about my daily activities. When I see or think of someone who is struggling, I send up a prayer for them right then, but it seems the person needing prayer more often than not is me. I'm always getting in some kind of predicament that I need assistance in handling.

Prayers in church vary as greatly as the people who attend. Often the pastor or someone chosen will pray aloud for the entire congregation. We can listen carefully and if in agreement, say 'Amen' at the end or we can always pray silently ourselves. One thing we do not want to do is let someone else do the praying for us. God is interested in the sincere desire of each heart, not just the ones who, seemingly, do it the best.

YOU CAN'T OUTGIVE GOD

The economy has been an important issue in our country for the last several months. Someone said recently, "The Bible doesn't say much about the economy, does it?"

In response I said it really has quite a bit to say about money. In fact, **Randy Alcorn**, in his book **'Money, Possessions and Eternity"** says there are twice as many verses devoted to money (about 2,350 of them) than to faith and prayer combined. I think this says that God was serious about how we handle what we have. My knowledge is limited on this subject so I recommend you read Mr. Alcorn's book. He makes some extremely valid points.

From the beginning of creation we know that God was concerned about the motivation of our giving because of the story of Cain and Abel's offerings to Him in Genesis 4:1-15.

He was also very explicit about the different offerings his people were to bring on special days and for different reasons. He knew that it was for their welfare that they allow Him to be their God and have first place in their lives. Their offerings were to be the first fruits of their labor meaning the best. The first place in the Bible that a tithe is mentioned is in Genesis 14:20. In Genesis 28:22; Leviticus 27:30-32 and Numbers 18:26 it mentions that our tithe should be a tenth of our labor.

In Malachi 3: 6-12 he speaks of robbing God if we do

not pay our tithes to him and at the same time cheating ourselves out of blessings because He is a sovereign God and ultimately in charge of our success or failure.

God is more interested in the attitude that we have about giving than in how much we give. The ninth chapter of II Corinthians is concerning generosity and how if we give generously and with a cheerful heart we will reap much good and if we give sparingly and grudgingly we will reap sparingly. Yet, we cannot give with the intention of getting back more because that would be for the wrong reason. Jesus said in Matthew 23:23, *"Woe unto you, scribes and Pharisees, hypocrites! For you pay titles of mint and anise and cumin, and have omitted the weightier matters of the law, judgment, mercy, and faith; these ought you to have done and not to leave the other undone."*

Many who believe in socialism, Marxism, Communism, etc., rally against Christians and accuse them of not caring about people who are poor. They promote free programs and distribution of wealth that sound good and the poor love them for it. The problem is that this only enables people to continue in their sinful lifestyles that cause poverty. The vicious cycle remains in place. Only God can change man's heart and that is what Christianity teaches. When the heart is changed it changes our actions that created the poverty that causes the problem in the first place.

The reason the ism's philosophies are embraced by so many seemingly good people is they think they can change society without giving up their own sins and be able to do things their way instead of God's way. It doesn't work as proven in the Garden of Eden and down through the ages.

Sometimes people like to say the Bible says that money is the root of all evil but it really says in I Timothy 6:9-10 *"For the love of money is the root of all kinds of evil."* . . . and it is.

Another well known verse is from Matthew 19:24.

Jesus said, *"Again I tell you, it is easier for a camel to go through the eye of a needle than for a rich man to enter the kingdom of God."* He follows this statement with *"With man this is impossible, but with God nothing is impossible."*

I have heard it said, 'Money makes a terrible master, yet it makes a good servant to those who have the right master __God. I think that is the secret.

It's an established fact that people of faith are the major contributors to charities and the building of institutions such as hospitals and schools that further the well being of our citizens, our culture and our country.

It is also well known that many times the people who give the most say the least about it. There is a good reason for this.

Jesus gave his disciples a tremendous amount of good instructions in the 5th, 6th and 7th chapters of the Book of Matthew. For Bible scholars these verses are referred to as 'The Sermon on the Mount.' In chapter 6, verses 1-4, He says, *"Be careful not to do your acts of righteousness before men, to be seen by them. If you do you will have no reward from your Father in heaven. So when you give to the needy, do not announce it with trumpets, as the hypocrites do in the synagogues and on the streets, to be honored by men. I tell you the truth, they have received their reward in full. But when you give to the needy, do not let your left hand know what your right hand is doing, so that your giving may be in secret. Then your Father who sees what is done in secret will reward you."*

CHURCH TRADITIONS

We attended Smiths Grove Baptist Church for about twenty years and experienced many ups and downs there. As with most small churches the traditions are strongly engrained into the minds and hearts of the people whose families have filled the pews throughout more than one generation. As with the majority of things, this can be good and bad.

When people have a 'home' church to which they feel emotionally attached, it gives them a sense of security. They form many positive connections that will remain with them all through their lives and serve as reminders of their past. The danger is that nostalgia and family traditions will become their religion and God's spirit will have no room in their lives. When we do something long enough and often enough, it will seem like the best and only thing that we should do. Our spiritual lives become stagnant and of no useful purpose in the Kingdom of God. This is what happened to the Pharisees and Sadducees in Jesus day. Then when Jesus came onto the scene, even though he was the awaited one, the very Son of God, they did not recognize him or accept his teachings. It was different from what they were used to. I have already stated how difficult it is to change our thinking as well as our actions.

When we started attending Smiths Grove Baptist Church I was pretty naïve and I don't think I had any inkling about how different my thinking was from the people already there. It was on the heels of my 'enlightenment' as to what a major part the Holy Spirit plays in the life of a Christian and I was excited about sharing my newfound knowledge with anyone who would listen. I wanted everyone to know what was available to them as a Christian. Because of this I was very outspoken in our Sunday school class and anywhere else I was allowed to speak. In later years one of our best friends that we got to know at that time told me he thought I was a radical. I really did not see myself as a radical but looking back I suppose he was right when I was compared to the thinking of the rest of the congregation.

Smiths Grove Baptist Church is one of the oldest organizations in a town of about one thousand people. In past years it was more of an aristocratic town with a normal school for girls and other prestigious institutions. It's base was the railroad as was many small towns in that era. Bowling Green, ten miles south, was a river town and larger. When both the railroad and the river were replaced by cars and trucks for transportation and commerce the small railroad towns lost their importance for commerce, as did Smiths Grove. The Baptist church was one of the first churches established in the town and the families were well engrained in its tradition. It was probably the most outstanding, as well, making the members additionally proud of their heritage. The people had become wealthy enough to build a beautiful building with some of the prettiest stained glass windows seen anywhere in the country. They had added extra space for education, built a parsonage next door to the church and were able to pay their pastor well for full-time service. I suppose because of this most of the people felt it was the duty of the pastor to be responsible for not only preaching and taking care of the parishioners but also to take care of leading the worship in song, prayers and teaching of doctrine. Maybe, because of this, the Board of Deacons saw it their duty to make sure he did what the church wanted because they were paying him well. In other words, he worked for them. Another thing I noticed was that hardly anyone brought their Bible to services. This was very noticeable to me because I was extremely interested in what mine said, especially at that time. In all probability I could have been compared to the old proverb, "A new broom sweeps fanatically clean."

I've already told you about the church where we came from. The members were used to doing many things themselves in the absence of a pastor who was only there, more or less, for the preaching on Sunday and business meetings. Even the young adults had been given the opportunity to lead the devotional at prayer meetings and express their thoughts in testimonials during worship. Everyone was taught to pray aloud and was given the opportunity. I remember one time some friends of ours who were members of the Church of Christ went with us to a revival service. They were aghast at the custom we had of everyone gathering into the altar at the same time and praying aloud simultaneously. I don't know where the custom originated but the viewpoint we had was that we were not praying to be heard by others, we were praying to God and he could hear and understand us all at the same time. Our friends were disturbed because they could not understand what anyone was saying. I suppose that would have been a bit confusing if I had been in their place and thought that was the purpose of it.

Another custom I remember was called a 'fellowship in the altar'. All who were Christians gathered into the middle of the room in front of the stage where the podium was and shook hands with each other. I believe this was supposed to help us love one another more and maybe it did. One of my memories of it was the unusual kinds of handshakes different people had. They ranged from hearty and strong to weak and limp like a dishrag or a dead fish. Some historians believe Christians substituted the handshake for the 'holy kiss' that Paul encouraged the early Christians to do in his letters to them. He ends four of his letters with 'greet each other with a holy kiss' and Peter ends one of his with 'greet each other with the kiss of love'. Whatever the reason, in America the handshake continues to be a greeting of good will anywhere we are and we can use all of that we can get!

One part of the doctrine of the church where I came from that I think some of the people at Smiths Grove Church were concerned about was the idea that General Baptist doctrine teaches that it is possible for a person to 'fall from grace'. Southern Baptists firmly believe that 'once you are saved, you are forever and always saved'. Both denominations base their beliefs on different passages of scripture. Once again, this is something that divides Christians and pleases Satan greatly. I, of course, leaned toward the way I was taught before my thorough study of the Bible. Afterwards, I could understand both teachings but had no problem with either because the Bible taught sufficient doctrine in many other ways. If we applied all of it, the dividing issue would take care of itself. I still believe some of the best advice I ever heard concerning this issue came from Roger Littrell, a dearly beloved General Baptist pastor.

He said, "Get right, live right, and die right, and you won't have to worry about it."

Again, both churches are extreme in their thinking about the doctrine of the other on this issue.

The Southern Baptists think that General Baptists believe if you commit any type of sin you are lost again.

This is not necessarily so. They believe when you sin that you need to ask (sincerely) to be forgiven for that sin because the Bible says no sin shall enter the kingdom of God. They do believe if you completely turn your back on God and reject Jesus as your savior that you can finally be lost.

The General Baptists sometimes think that Southern Baptists believe the only important thing is that people be saved and then it doesn't matter what they do or how they live because they cannot lose their salvation no matter what they do. This is true, to a point, but not in the way supposed. They believe if you are saved, your sins, past and future, are forgiven and covered by the blood of Jesus and because of his grace you will be saved. The Bible says that when we are saved we are sealed by the Holy Spirit, and that seal cannot be broken. If you completely turn your back on God and reject Jesus totally as your savior, they believe you were never truly saved to begin with. If you are truly saved, the Holy Spirit will convict you when you sin and bring you to the point of repentance.

So you see, it really isn't as cut and dried as either group of Christians would have you believe who want to be more right than the other one. I might say, I am a little concerned about anyone that has this attitude in the first place. It is just another tactic that Satan uses to poison our minds and hearts to keep us from growing the Kingdom of God here on earth. If we will sincerely seek God's guidance through his word, via the Holy Spirit, this will not be a problem for us.

In spite of my having a different background and being a bit of a radical, I was asked to teach the Young Adult Sunday School Class that Tom and I were members of. I suppose if I have a spiritual gift it would be teaching. I love doing it and really have a desire to lead others to want to learn things that will change their lives for the better. Another lady and I took turns teaching on Sunday morning for several years. During this time I was asked to teach the older youth in a Vacation Bible School. The pastor suggested that we have the first class meeting at our house and have home-made ice cream and some type of recreation appropriate for their age. As the children get older they think they have outgrown VBS and we thought this might make them feel better about it. It turned out to be a good idea and was very successful. Because of this we decided to keep on having Bible study at our house for anyone that was interested on a weekly basis. We had it several weeks and attendance was from twenty to thirty people.

After a few weeks, I felt a little bad about not having it at church so decided to change the meeting place to the fellowship hall in the back of the church. By doing this I felt we would be accomplishing the same thing and supporting the church as well. We lost a few people but the attendance continued to be pretty good. In fact, it was on a Wednesday evening and many times the attendance at our Bible study was greater than the regular attendance at prayer meeting in the sanctuary assembly. I think this was possibly the reason the leaders of the church asked us to discontinue the Bible study in the back.

This action by the church leaders was very difficult for me to understand. I sincerely felt that a lot of good was being done because there was much interest from many of the people in the group in learning the scriptures. I remember shedding many tears about the situation and asking God "Why?" My answer came from the scripture. It was from I Peter 3: 8-17 where he talks about suffering for doing good. I guess this was my first and most difficult persecution that I had experienced thus far as a Christian. The most difficult part was that it came from other Christians.

We did cease the Bible studies at church on Wednesday evenings but continued to have them on Tuesday evenings at our home. This went on for several years and different people attended at times as well as a core group of us who became rather close. I still count them as some of my closest friends today. We studied through several books of the Bible, using no literature, just reading the scriptures and discussing them as a group. I don't know as I was qualified to teach except only by having the Holy Spirit as my help and guide which, in my opinion, is the best qualification of all. I'm sure I learned as much as anyone else because I was sincerely seeking to know.

A new pastor came some years later and asked us to move the Bible study back to church because he felt the Wednesday night group needed us. We gave up the Bible study and did as he asked. Sometime later he admitted that it had been a mistake to do this, but God forgives mistakes and makes all things work for the good of those who love the Lord and who have been called according to his purpose. (Romans 8:28.)

Another incident happened that I may not have used good judgment in. One of the lady teachers at Smiths Grove Baptist Church took a group of the young children from the church to see the movie 'Kindergarten Cop.' I did not have any children in the group but parents in my class did and they came to me, concerned, because they did not approve of the church supporting a film with profanity and violence in it. I went with a group of the parents to meet with the deacons who were the ruling body of the church at that time, and the teacher who had taken them. She was very upset to be called 'before the deacons' as she put it and reprimanded. At the time I did not see it in that way, I just thought using the church's money and name to support this type of movie was not a good action to take. Looking back I think we may have already been aggravated because the church had just voted down a man to be pastor that the pastor search committee had recommended. One of the parents that was so upset, and myself, were on that committee. I later had to apologize to the lady for offending her because that was not my intention.

However, because of the movie incident, and shortly following, at an evening service, the lady stood in front of the church and rebuked us quite adamantly and said we needed to get the devil out of the church. (I think she was talking about me.) Years later she apologized to me and I know, on my part, there are no hard feelings, and I hope none on hers either.

I have often said that small churches teach their young pastors who are new in the ministry as much as the pastor teaches them. It may well have been that sometimes Smiths Grove Baptist Church has been this type of church. I still believe this concept to be true. Physical years do not always make a person wiser or more spiritually mature but most of the time it helps. Experience is still one of the greatest teachers. Now that I am older, I see that, but, I probably would not have believed it in my earlier years. I remember a line from the play, "The Matchmaker" by Thornton Wilder that I performed in one summer in repertory at Horse Cave Theatre that has a lot of merit. It stated, "A fellow doesn't know a thing until he's forty." That is perhaps a bit embellished but it usually does take several years for wisdom to solidify. Now don't mistake wisdom for knowledge. Knowledge is information; wisdom is knowing how to use what we know effectively. Knowledge is much more easily acquired and remembered in our younger years. How I wish I had realized this more fully when I was in the throes of youth. It sometimes seems that most of my lessons have usually come 'after the fact' or by 'learning from my mistakes.' It is then too late for me to benefit from them and not many who would, want to hear my opinions. Even so, not everyone ages the same because I will have to admit that some people do not seem to grow wiser with the years, and that is sad. There are also exceptions to the young being wise such as Job's young friend, Elihu, who gave him better advice than he received from his older friends, Eliphaz, Bildad, and Zophar. I surely believe that the Holy Spirit can make a person wise at any age and also in cases of mental impairment. God can certainly give wisdom to whom or whatever he chooses. Remember when he gave it to the donkey that Balaam was riding? You can read about it in Numbers, chapter twenty two.

A church that God uses to 'grow ministers' certainly is not a bad thing. The Bible tells us that some of His vessels are made of silver and gold and some are made of wood and clay but they are all equally important in His kingdom. This idea is not in keeping with the world's standard, and I'm afraid, with a lot of Christians. The twelfth chapter of the book of Romans explains this in a very comprehensive way. If all members of a congregation took this concept to heart, there would be no jealousy or division and everyone would enjoy using the special gift that God has given them to promote the Kingdom of God on earth. Of course, Satan does not like that idea at all, thus he uses every weapon at his disposal to keep us from putting it into practice as he does all the rest of the scriptures.

I enjoyed teaching the young adult Sunday school class at Smiths Grove Baptist Church and did so for several years – long enough for us to become the 'older' adult Sunday school class. I became very attached to being a part of the church congregation and believed that I was needed to help the people enlarge their thinking about God and how he works in our lives. I performed different duties at various times when I felt someone needed to do them. I did some things that were certainly not my gift such as playing the piano and leading the choir in practice. Every church seems to go through cycles of growth and loss of members. We were no different. Part of the time we attended Smiths Grove Baptist Church it was at low ebb. I even prepared the bulletin for the Sunday morning services for a period of time when we were without a regular pastor. Looking back, I'm not sure I should have done all the things I did because I wasn't qualified but I felt they needed to be done and was willing to try. Sometimes it is still difficult for me to determine if I should attempt to do something I see that needs to be done or to wait on God to show me for sure if that is what He wants me to do. By nature, I will just "do it myself" but more and more, my spirit says 'wait on the Lord.' I am reminded that '*His ways are not our ways, and they are as far apart as the heavens are above the earth.*' Isa 55:8-9 (NIV) Therefore, I have come to believe that we must make sure we are doing it His way and not ours.

I have never been a person to depend wholly on the church I attend to fill all of my spiritual needs. Most of my life I have been an avid reader and seeker of the truth. Many writers have provided spiritual knowledge and inspiration to me through the years. When I delivered the mail I listened to three different ministers on the Christian radio station as well as many audio tapes that fed my spirit every morning as I drove around the route. I always enjoyed going to different churches when given the opportunity, such as when we went on family vacations. While attending Smiths Grove Baptist Church, I heard that good things were happening at Hillvue Heights Church in Bowling Green. Since I was teaching at the time and did not want to miss service at Smiths Grove I figured out that I could go to the early morning service at Hillvue and get back in time for the regular services at Smiths Grove. It worked out great and I continued the practice for quite some time. After awhile, my husband,

Tom, went to Hillvue with me and really liked the service there. He especially liked the young, dynamic pastor who preached with a flare for entertainment and could keep him awake. Eventually, he began going there full time and I continued going to Smiths Grove because I was teaching. I had done what others have often been guilty of, gotten attached to my warm spot and did not want to move over. We convince ourselves that no one else can do the job, or at least do it as well, but that is seldom true. God can and will always raise up someone else to stand in the gap when we move over whatever the reason, good or bad.

Tom and I continued to go our separate ways on Sunday morning for several years and perhaps, at the time, it was for the best because we both needed space. I really do not recommend this to others because worshipping together is one of the best things a family can do but in our situation, God had mercy on us and provided a way out of our self centeredness.

It was after I served on a committee to find a new pastor and felt that God had sent the one He chose for us that I was led to leave Smiths Grove and go to Hillvue with my husband. I did it, but I really did not want to. I had always believed that God works in all churches if we allow Him to, both big and small and we should not all want to go to the big ones who seemingly have the most to offer. I still believe this, but in my case, I think God saw the need to break my will and convince me that He is in control. Hopefully, I have learned my lesson, but I'm sure I will forget at times as we humans are so prone to do.

I appreciate all the people that we worshipped with at Smiths Grove church and thank them for being patient with me. I certainly learned a lot during the time we attended there. They all have a special place in my heart that will remain forever. It is always good to go back and visit and see God's work continuing on.

MY PHYSICAL HEALING

During the time we attended church in Smiths Grove I experienced some very severe physical health problems with my colon. This was unusual for me because I have always been reasonably healthy. I went to different doctors and they treated me for amebic dysentery, colitis, and even suggested that I might have Chrons disease for which there was no cure. They put me on smooth foods, no roughage or spicy foods and other diets. I took many kinds of medicine but none seemed to help. In fact, the medication made me feel terrible and created negative side effects. It was the most medicine I had taken in my entire life and made me feel the worst. This went on for two or three years.

One day I was reading in the book of James, chapter five, verses 11-15. It says, *"Is anyone among you suffering? He should keep on praying about it. And those who have reason to be thankful should continually be singing praises to the Lord."*

"Is anyone sick? He should call for the elders of the church and they should pray over him and pour a little oil upon him, calling on the Lord to heal him. And their prayer, if offered in faith, will heal him, for the Lord will make him well; and if his sickness was caused by some sin, the Lord will forgive him." (TLB)

I had certainly prayed about my illness and had even fasted for three days without food or drink, but seemed to get no answer. As I read this scripture, I was moved to follow the instructions.

The next Sunday morning, I carried with me a small bottle of olive oil from home. Each Sunday morning between Bible study and worship service the deacons met together in the pastor's study for prayer. I asked my husband and one or two members from our Sunday school class to join me while I made my request. We joined the pastor and deacons; I read from my Bible the passage above and asked them to follow it. I gave the oil to the pastor and even though he looked a bit surprised, he took it and with his finger rubbed a little on my forehead. After praying, there was kind of an uncomfortable silence as we went into the sanctuary to worship. At the next deacon's meeting, it was decided that they would not practice this act of service anymore because they did not feel it went along with the doctrine of the church.

I did not feel any different but I believed that God would heal me because of my obedience to follow his word. Two or three days later as I was standing in my kitchen peeling potatoes for dinner, I unexpectedly noticed that my whole body was in a strain as I rushed to peel the potatoes. The nerves and sinews in my legs, my body, my arms and hands were taut. I wasn't in any particular hurry but I was in such a habit of rushing that I did it automatically.

Suddenly the revelation came to me. I was stressing my body all over continuously and that was what was causing the problem with my colon. If you had asked me if I was a nervous person or if I was under a lot of stress, my answer would have been "No." It was something I had developed over the years and was totally unaware of. I was the type of personality that thought a person should be productive all the time, that things needed to be done a certain way and to get them done that way, I needed to do them. It is no wonder I was stressed!

From that day on I set about learning to relax and the challenge proved successful. The healing did as well. I took no more medication, did not go back to any doctor and my problems with my colon disappeared. I have been able to eat any kind of food I want to and have not had any signs of the illness. That was fifteen to twenty years ago. Praise the Lord!! I give him the glory and the credit.

THE UNEXPECTED VISITOR

It was a day quite like any other day on the farm where Tom and I and our three sons lived. Activities began fairly early and each one went about the business of the day with few expectations other than to accomplish the tasks before them. That is not to say, life was boring because where we lived seemed to be a prime spot for attracting people from many walks of life. Few days passed without something or someone unusual breaking the monotony of labor and enriching our limited hours. This day proved to be no different and was etched in my memory demanding frequent reminders.

In the afternoon I walked out to the workshop where several of the guys were either working or loafing and to my surprise there was a young man in a black leather jacket sitting on an empty, upside down five gallon paint bucket. He was a stranger to me and seemed to be to the rest of them. Since I am a person who believes everyone has an interesting story, I often start conversations with people I do not know providing it is a secure situation and I see no danger in doing so. As I questioned the stranger, I found he had been walking along the road that runs by our place and had stopped for a drink of water. He told me his name and I have forgotten it. I think part of it was 'Lee'. After a bit of conversation, I asked him if he was hungry and offered him a bologna sandwich. He took me up on the offer and followed me to the house to collect. He sat down at the kitchen table and as I made his sandwich, I could not resist the urge to ask him if he was a Christian. I don't remember his answer, but I remember his question. He looked at me with the clearest, deepest, haunting eyes I have ever seen and said, "Do you know what Isaiah 53:6 means?"

His question took me totally by surprise. I'm sure I must have shown it by my expression. My second surprise was that I was familiar with the scripture and knew what it meant. I told him what I thought it meant and do not remember what he said. All I can remember are those unforgettable eyes. After he had eaten two bologna sandwiches, my husband, Tom, drove him to Smiths Grove and let him out at the truck stop where he figured he could catch a ride to his destination. He said he was headed to Rawletts which was probably twenty to twenty-five miles away. I never saw him again but I have often wondered if he could have been an angel unawares, such as the Bible speaks about. (Hebrews 13:2

A WOMAN'S PLACE

I mentioned earlier that my maternal grandfather and grandmother were charter members of the church where I grew up. That was in 1904, over a century ago, and a woman was a charter member! Does that surprise you? Now that I think of it, it kind of surprises me, but it shouldn't. I suppose the reason is because of all the ha-la-ba-loo that has surrounded the liberation of women in my lifetime. Growing up, and as a young woman, I never had a problem with it. Women led in prayer and were in charge of the devotional for prayer service on Wednesday evening as often as men. It was only later in my life when I was probably having a little too much influence in the church where we attended that it kind of became a problem. I taught an adult Bible class of both men and women and some of the members of the church did not think a woman should teach a class with adult men in it. I understood their concern because of the scripture in I Timothy 2:12 but I can honestly say that I had no thought of having any authority over anyone, male or female. My desire and intent was to inspire and encourage the people in the class to study and search the scriptures and allow the Holy Spirit to work in their lives so that our church could be salt and light in the community. I believed then, and still do, that the role of the church is to preach and teach the good news to all that haven't heard it and to nurture the ones that have experienced the new spiritual birth to maturity so that they may influence others. My theory is, "The more salt and light in our world, the less evil and darkness."

I believe the scripture that says a woman must be silent in the church and if they wanted to know anything to ask their husbands was in the circumstances for which it was written. (I Corinthians 14:34&35) In the Corinthian church there was a lot of confusion during their services about speaking in tongues, etc. Paul was attempting to instruct them on who should speak and when. Seemingly some of the women were guilty of abusing the privilege. In that period of time the status of most women was very low compared to men. They were not allowed to study and it was assumed that they did not have enough knowledge or experience to teach or even speak to a situation. Giving them the chance to learn from the men was an amazing opportunity for them. I Timothy 2: 11&12 also speak to this issue. If we take this scripture literally, and read the following three verses, we must also believe that a woman cannot be saved if she does not bear children. (Verse 15) We surely do not believe that, do we?

As far as I am concerned the Bible speaks very clearly on the matter in other places. Paul mentions in Acts 18:24-26, Priscilla, and her husband, Aquila, who taught the great teacher Apollos. He highly commends them in Acts 16:3 as he does several other women in the following verses (6-15). Euodia and Syntyche are another two women that Paul encouraged in Philippians 4:2. Anna, the prophetess was given a special privilege in Luke 2:36 and Philip, the evangelist, had four daughters that prophesied. In the Old Testament, Deborah was one of the righteous judges of Israel, Esther was used by God to save the Jews and Ruth had a book written about her. Surely we cannot say that women cannot or should not play an important role in carrying out the Great Commission. (Matthew 28:18-20)

It says in Galatians 3: 26-29, (NIV) *"You are all sons of*

God through faith in Christ Jesus, for all of you who were baptized into Christ have clothed yourselves with Christ. There is neither Jew nor Greek, slave nor free, male nor female, for you are all one in Christ Jesus. If you belong to Christ, then you are Abraham's seed, and heirs according to the promise."

Jesus also told the Samaritan woman at the well in John 4: 23&24, *"Yet a time is coming and has now come when the true worshipers will worship the Father in spirit and truth, for they are the kind of worshipers the Father seeks. God is spirit, and his worshipers must worship in spirit and in truth."* (NIV)

My limited understanding is that spiritual beings are not known or acknowledged by their gender, therefore, that is not as important to the God of the universe as it seems to be to us mere mortals. It is only in the physical realm that He gave male and female special places to fill and guidelines for doing so. When we are worshiping or attending to the affairs of God, we should be "in the spirit' or, at least, controlled by it, in order to correctly understand the scriptures and know the mind of God concerning the matters at hand. If a woman does not meet these criteria, as was the case in Paul's letter to the Corinthian church, she should keep quiet and not cause disorder and chaos in the church.

However, this is also true of a man. In our society today, one could probably point to facts that show men who are leaders in the church constitute a higher percentage of moral failure than women do. I have not done research on the matter and am not sure there is any, but the idea might be worth considering.

I say all of this, and yet, I do believe that God placed man in authority over all his creation, including woman, and it is his place to assume the responsibility of protecting and providing leadership in caring for it. I have never had a desire to be a 'preacher' but I do have the desire to see God's people, male and female, know him better by a thorough study of the scriptures allowing the Holy Spirit to guide them in the understanding of it. I once attended a course written and taught on video by Kay Arthur which definitely assured me that a woman can "preach" as well as a man. She does not refer to herself as a preacher and would probably object to it if I did, but she speaks with such passion that one cannot help but be inspired by her teaching. As far as I understand, that is what people who speak for God are supposed to do.

On the other hand, the majority of my teachers have been men and I appreciate every one of them. One of the most capable teachers I have ever learned under is Del Tackett who teaches 'The Truth Project" on video. His knowledge and presentation is superb, the skill he exhibits is outstanding and his passion is inspiring.

I believe genuine Christians know and recognize that God can use anyone or anything He wishes to bring about his plan for mankind. If I am not mistaken, in the Bible he used the lowly donkey to get Balaam's attention (Numbers 22: 21-39) and a rooster to remind Peter of his arrogance. (Luke: chapter 22) It seems to me that the first qualification needs to be availability; then, he will show us how to prepare ourselves for the task or give us the grace and capability to do it. I believe He uses people many times when they are not even aware of it.

Since I have brought up the subject of Christian men, I might as well elaborate on that as well.

Our pastor said recently that our church was one of the few who have more males attend than females. I rejoice in this. I am so glad to see men assume their place as spiritual leader of their home. If husbands and fathers do not set the example for their children and be the husband the scriptures teach them to be, the family is in trouble.

If the family is in trouble, so is the nation. Fathers are important in teaching their sons to be men and in being an example of the kind of husband their daughters should choose. How I wish men everywhere would realize what a vital place they have in our society. How I wish our culture would put more emphasis on being good fathers and husbands than on how much money one can make or how powerful one can become. In the halls of power, whether business, politics, education or whatever, it seems something has to take second place and too often it is the home and family. It used to be true with men, now it is also true with working women. I am not against women working but when I had my first, and only, fulltime job in my early fifties it was not hard to see how much time, energy and attention a job requires. I hurt for any woman who has children and must work fulltime, especially if she is the major caretaker. There are always exceptions when husbands are willing to do as much or more than their share in the process. I rejoice to see fathers encouraged to take an increased role in parenthood. Teaching and caring for young children is one of the most important jobs in life and one of the most rewarding. Why should men miss out on all the fun? It only takes about twenty years out of a person's life and then one can work all they want to. I'm afraid many children today have not been taught, they have been allowed to grow up on their own and our culture has changed because of it – and not for the better.

In the church I grew up in it was very common for the entire family to attend but in many churches in the last part of the twentieth century this was not the norm. Somehow it became popular for men to stay home and let their wives attend and take the children. RED LIGHT FLASHING!!! It doesn't work. "If it isn't important enough for Daddy to go to church, it must not be very

WHAT IS ART?

Charles Colson, in his book 'Burden of Truth,' expressed his sentiments concerning how we Christians should be leading the world in the field of art. I was enthralled by his thoughts because the arts have been of special interest to me throughout my life. I have always loved and appreciated music, singing, books and the theatre. When our sons were young we sang as a family group for our church and a few others in the surrounding community. It was when they were young enough not to be embarrassed by it! Of course, we were in no way professional, mind you, but it made a good memory for me, and hopefully, them as well.

We also traveled to several towns around the state to see outdoor dramas on our mini vacations.

Later on I even did a little acting in repertory theatre one summer season at what was then the Horse Cave Theatre in Horse Cave, Ky. I have also taken playwright lessons in the winter months there. Writing became an inspiration when my junior high teacher wrote an encouraging word on a short story I had written as an assignment. It must have begun when I developed a hunger for reading all of the books that the library book mobile brought periodically to the small community elementary school that I attended. No matter what they were, I read them. I precisely remember reading many biographies of past presidents. Growing up we did not have many books to read. Every family I knew had the Bible and it was the most important by far. 'Little Women' by Louisa Mae Alcott was the first fiction book that I remember reading and enjoying tremendously. I identified with the sister "Jo", who was a writer, and longed to be just like her. See how art can influence an impressionable young mind.

I believe the arts can move us to open our spirit and grasp more of what God wants us to know about His world and its' people.

The problem is that I am appalled at what has become recognized as good art in today's world. Much of today's 'art' doesn't have to move you, or make you think, or even make sense at all. Even much comedy is not funny, just silly. Maybe the purpose is to make us stretch our imaginations in order to be able to laugh at it or understand it. The major idea seems to be that it hasn't been thought of or done before. Another criterion, that Mr. Colson mentioned was that if it was done by a well known and accepted artist in the art world it could be a white, blank, sheet of poster board and if he or she said it was art, no one would argue with them.

It is a very sad thing, in my opinion, that our culture has allowed this to happen.

Many of the plays, movies, songs and books written today are vulgar, nonsensical and ludicrous. I know, I know, that is only my opinion, but I have a right to have it, and to express it, and I think one might be surprised how many people would agree with me if the multitudes were not fearful of being called or assumed to be ignorant. I am certainly cautious about spending my time and money for seeing a movie or play, or even reading material, before I review it thoroughly. My mind and time are too valuable to waste!

Many playwrights think a play has to be crude, rude and crazy to be considered of any value. The sad truth is that this is what is promoted by the media the majority of the time, and thus, many people will pay their money to see them.

I am aware that many who consider themselves

professionals will say that I am not qualified to have a creditable opinion and do not know what I am talking about. If they are aware of my opinions at all, they will say it is uneducated and has no merit in intelligent circles. That is their right and on some points they might be close to the truth! I am taking steps to rectify that. I have recently signed up for another course at the university. The name of it is "Living With Art," eighth edition, by Mark Getelin. I think I'm going to enjoy it; but, so far, it has only reinforced my opinion.

I think it is high time Christians took back the art world. If you will look at ancient art you will see that it used to be so. Art was to extol the Creator and display the beauty of the world and the creatures and people in it. The first account of artistic ability we have was in the book of Genesis when God gave Bezalel and Oholiab the ability to create art for decorating the tabernacle for His glory. He gives us gifts of creativity today for the same purpose. I'm afraid He must be disappointed in what many of us are doing with them. One of my favorite quotes is "The Spirit Makes the Master" that was coined by Dr. Henry Hardin Cherry of Bowling Green, KY as one of the mottos for Western Kentucky University. This includes art and the outcome is determined by which spirit is in control.

I believe the church world should take an active part in determining what constitutes good art. No one should be able to express or recognize beauty better than the ones who know the creator of it on an intimate level. As Christians, we should display beauty in everything we do. Any type of work is an art if one makes it so. Taking pride in what we do, whether digging ditches or building great edifices is the way to contribute our personal art to the world we live in. There are not many females who have not cooked a meal or at least a part of a meal at one time or another. Cooking is an art and may I dare say, one that is probably enjoyed the most by the largest number of people.

Great anthems of the past were written for spiritual enlightenment and enjoyment. Songs were for fun and relaxation, not filled with sexual innuendos, negative connotations and profanity. Plays were written to teach us virtue and move us to seek after what is good and noble. Even children's stories had a moral to them.

What happened? How did we get to this place? Is this where we want to be? Is this the world we want our children to grow up in?

With all the resources available to us, why does our culture seem to resemble the Dark Ages in so many ways?

We live in the land of the free, and we are free. Free to choose better than this. Is the reason we are at this place in our culture because of the choices we have made? Is this how smart we are? Will our freedom bring destruction upon us? The answer is in the Bible. We are descendants of Adam and Eve. They had everything they could want and look at the choices they made. What happened to them because of it? Without following the teachings of the Bible and guidance from above we will always choose what is harmful to us in the long run. We have gotten so smart that we think we know what is better but we are being deceived. God is light and without Him, there is darkness, and darkness is evil. I am convinced that the evil one is behind all of this decay that is taking place in our culture.

It was President John Quincy Adams, 1776, that said, "It is religion and morality alone which can establish the principles upon which freedom can securely stand."

I think time has proven him right.

Don't think I am a negative person. I certainly am not. I believe whatever happens in this world God will take care of His children and supply our needs if we seek Him. I am also a realist. I read in the scriptures where God's people turned aside from following Him and did what they wanted to do, and, every time, they destroyed themselves. I believe we would do well to read, study and heed the scriptures once again as the people did that founded and organized this great country of ours. There is no doubt in my mind this was the reason we enjoyed such success and world prominence for 200 years. Rome did too, and what happened to it?

In fact, I recently read an interesting statement from Francis A. Schaeffer's book, **How Should We Then Live?** He quoted **Edward Gibbon (1737-1794) in his 'Decline and Fall of the Roman Empire'** as saying "The five attributes that marked Rome at its end was; first, a mounting love of show and luxury (that is, affluence); second, a widening gap between the very rich and the very poor (this could be among countries in the family of nations as well as in a single nation); third, an obsession with sex; fourth, freakishness in the arts, masquerading as originality, and enthusiasms pretending to be creativity; and fifth, an increased desire to live off the state. Does that ring any bells for you?

To be completely honest, Dr. Colson's article is what prompted me to finish this book and include some of my poems in it. The following are two that expresses my thoughts about art that was written in 2004.

Art, I Love

I see great paintings that stir the soul
I touch sculptures from times of old
I hear stirring music in symphony
And long for the creator to be me.

I stroke an animal of silk soft fur,
I hear the song of the mockingbird
I gaze into a cool crystal stream
And fall at the feet of the creator.

I walk along in fresh turned soil
I feel dirt squish between my toes
I breathe deeply the earthy aroma
And marvel how a green thing grows!

A tree is a miracle, a work of art,
Fed and designed by the hand of God
Each leaf placed in its special place
Creating beauty, balance, and space--

Not only lovely but playing its' part
Shading me from the sizzling sun,
Providing a breeze for my sweaty face
Cooling my body like an art of grace--

I lift my song with heartfelt glee
I hear a story at grandfather's knee
Art that endures the passing of time
I treasure ardently, as age-old wine.

Inspiration

As water flows from height to depth
Without effort, pain or resistance;
So drains the dregs from my soul,
Leaving bare, the heart, an empty vessel--

Like objects, without gravity, ascends,
Mental musings escape my mind, floating
Nonchalantly toward the heavens,
Freeing space for fragments of time
To splash her colors in prisms of glory--

Creating ideas, yet unfathomed;
Dreaming images of mysterious shadows;

Hearing melodious music of virgin birth;
Bringing new life to smoldering timbers--

The Spirit explodes in bursts of fireworks,
Awing spectators for centuries yet to be
With creations from the mind of God,
To alter His world as He sees fit.

Great art comes from inspiration via the Holy Spirit
not from the mind being stretched by artificial stimulants
that blow it in untold directions. Another truth I have
discovered is that creative people sometimes appear to be
lazy and this may not be true. Quieting the mind may be
necessary in order for our creative juices to flow. It is hard
for the mind to unveil new ideas and thoughts if it is always
busy concentrating on the work at hand. What would an
American do if he or she were given three months off
from work with shelter, clothing and food provided but no
spending money or anywhere to spend it?

I would not be afraid to bet my last dollar that most
of us would be at our wit's end in less than a week. We
have forgotten how to be creative in occupying our time
productively on our own. No computers, no TV, no
books to read and no programmed activities. "What is
there left to do", you ask.

"What would you do?"

Let's think.

We could take a walk and enjoy the scenery,
contemplate the feel of the weather on our face and body,
study the plants, trees, rock formations and anything else
that nature provides for our pleasure. We could watch for
animals and study their habitat and life patterns by doing
it several days in a row at the same time of day. We could
study the heavens, the clouds, stars, planets, sun, moon,
wind and learn about how it works and creates different

weather conditions. This would take quite a bit of time. Visiting our neighbors would be nice. It might take some time to find someone at home but there would probably be several older, retired people plus handicapped or wealthy-capped people who just might be lonely and enjoy having someone to talk to. It might take some effort learning to really communicate with people who are out of our age range and culture but it might be an interesting adventure.

Is it possible that creativity is better developed when we have lots of time and the creation is sometimes more interesting if we have no money and have to use available resources in our environment. We could begin by remembering the early settlers in this country and how they managed to spend their spare time . . . what little they had of it!

One of the most inspiring times of my life was on a vacation Tom and I took to see the Badlands of South Dakota and the mountains around Mount Rushmore. When we stood at the base of Mount Rushmore I marveled at the idea of carving out of a huge, stone, mountain, the images of the four presidents, with only hand picks and chisels. Before it was finished, more modern tools were used but when Gutzon Borglum conceived the original dream they were not in the picture. What an idea! What a vision! What faith that it could be done!

I stood for a few minutes, transformed by my imagination of it all. After we left the site and drove through the mountains around Needlepoint I felt as if I was in a wonderland. The mountains seemed majestic to me.

The inspiring spirit did not leave me for a few days. The next morning around two o'clock I awoke and could not go back to sleep. It was then that I wrote the following poem.

Viewing Mount Rushmore

I stood at the foot of the mountain;
Gazing up, God's glory to see;
I felt the power of His majesty
Flowing out of His hand to me-

My heart stood still within me,
Yet leapt with a strong desire;
To know a God more fully,
Who greatness in man can inspire

To climb to the top of such mountains
And work to carve faces of men;
Seems not only a task foreboding,
But an impossible challenge to win.

Yes, greatness begins in a small way;
When the mind of man dares to dream
And believes in a God who gives us
The ability, the guts, the means!

I stand in awe of your presence;
The mountain's grandeur holds me still;
I long for the power of your spirit
To set free the greatness I feel.

How I would love to contribute
To your world in some small way,
That mankind may be inspired,
As I have been here today.

What can I do with so little?
What do I have in my hand?
Show me just what I can do
To be an inspiration to man-

A few men do great things,
Many do small things great;
Just show me what I can do
What contribution I can make.

Open my mind to your wisdom
Let my ears attend to your voice;
Make my heart willing to follow
Not my own will, but your choice.

While still under the same influence the following day, while we traveled toward home, I was still writing poetry. As my husband drove, I gazed up at the clouds and composed these poems.

Vacationing
We're leaving the Black Hills and mountains,
Driving into the bright rising sun;
We've tasted a bit of the glory
That God's mighty hand has done.

The clouds break on the horizon;
The winds left rain last night
Our bodies are refreshed and rested,
The world seems to be near right.

How important a time of refuge,
To leave the mundane behind,
And escape the burdens of labor,
If only for a portion of time.

To spend time alone together;
To nurture the love we contain;
Think new thoughts, See new things;
Feel the taste of freedom again.

We beheld your mountains of grandeur
And gazed upon the Badlands in awe;
We enjoyed the menagerie of animals
Becoming one with nature so raw.

The spirit is refreshed within us,
The soul has been lifted to know
That the God who made all this glory
Can be with us wherever we go.

A Possibility
When I look at the sky
I wish I could fly
Way up to a cloud
Where the thunder is loud
Where the birds glide by
Like a fox on the sly;

When they see me thy say,
"Oh, My, what a day"!
"You don't belong here.
You're not a bird, Dear,
You're much too bound,
Upon the ground,
By earth and things
To ever have wings"

Is it so? I asked.
Myself, aghast!
Is it possible for me
To ever be free
To fly above
The things I love
And be as free
As I want to be

Just for fun, I wrote this one about Tom. You would have to know him to appreciate it. He has never been a big conversationalist and many times that has frustrated me to no end but on that day nothing could dampen my spirit. These were the topics he had talked about while on that trip. As I read them again, I smile. They are so much 'man' interests!

Numbers

Tom loves to count,
Anyway it seems;
The number of things
Determines the means.
How many miles?
Look how much hay!
How many hours
Have we driven today?
What time is it?
How many miles till?
How many more gallons
Our gas tank to fill?
How many machines
To bale that much hay?
How many people live

Along this highway?
There must be five million
Rolls of baled hay;
Look at all the grain bins
And no grain to weigh;
How many people
Attended Godstock?
How many animals
In each little flock?
Three trailers pulled
Behind one truck;
One picture of that
Would be good luck;
One, two three,
Four, five, six, seven;
Without numbers, to Tom,
Would not be heaven.

A couple of years later we went west again and visited the Yellowstone National Park. I wrote this poem on that trip.

On The Road Again!
On the road
My husband and I
To see the sights
While passing by

Down the highway,
State by state,
No worries at all
Of being late

Our work aside
Open to fate
A time to enjoy
A vacation date

We travel along,
Trying not to miss
Anything of interest
In our time of bliss

The stately pines,
The graceful hills,
The placid lakes
All nature yields.

A place and time
Each one a throne
God made it all
His very own!

An amazing feat
This earth of His
Such wondrous beauty
The variety is

To see it all
So far, so near,
Makes one feel small
To Earth, so dear

So I must look
To God above
To recognize
The vastness of

His power so strong
His love so deep
May I to Him
My worship keep!

Nature has always been special to me, especially the woods. It may be because I spent a lot of time there as a child. Many days I walked through them going to find the cows and drive them up to be milked in the evenings. My brother and I spent hours roaming the woods on our small farm picking blackberries and gathering walnuts and hickory nuts. One of our favorite recreations was racing to climb barefoot up tall skinny saplings to see who could get almost to the top first and swing them over to land us on the ground.

Living in Kentucky gave me a special appreciation for the change in the seasons. The hills and mountains display magnificent splendor in all of them. Each season has a meaning of its own. Spring reminds me of the excitement of life and adventure; summer is lazy, fun filled and busy; autumn gives us an opportunity to enjoy the benefit of our labors and winter allows us a chance to slow our pace, enjoy memories, contemplate life's mysteries and get organized again for what is ahead.

Today there is a lot of talk about preventing global warming, protecting our environment and preserving our resources. This should be nothing new to Christians. God put humans in charge of the animals and all living things in the Garden of Eden. He gave us instructions on how to take care of them and use them for our welfare. Adam and Eve failed to heed His advice and things got messed up. They are even more messed up now because there are more humans and the majority of us are still in rebellion against doing things His way. We think our way is better.

Most Americans waste more that they use. Satan has convinced us that "The one with the most toys wins; the most fashionably dressed is the best looking and the most famous movie star celebrity is the happiest." Our fast paced lifestyle is to make all the money we can, so we can buy all of the things we can, to impress as many people as we can and spend all our time either letting it possess us by taking care of it or taking it to landfills so we can shop for more. When something is slightly worn or needs a little repair, the common consensus is 'it will be cheaper to throw it away and buy a new one.'

Much of the time we are in such a hurry doing all of this that we do not take time to enjoy any of it. "Waste not, want not," used to be the American mantra, now it seems to be "Spend all the money that we don't have so we can make more."

I'm sorry, but this does not sound like good sense to me.

On the other hand, our government wants us to curtail our energy use to cut down on carbons and tax us for doing it.

For many years I have recycled almost everything possible and tried to use up most items to their limit. I am made fun of for saving things like slightly used paper napkins for future use to wipe up spills, etc. from the floor. I feel it just makes good sense to take care of everything, including our natural resources.

I practice this because I feel it is God's creation and we should respect it, use it for His glory and our benefit and then not worry about global warming, etc. If mankind is smart enough to mess up God's world, He will stop us if He doesn't want it to happen. My faith is in God much more than any plan our government or anyone else can come up with. Al Gore's "Inconvenient Truth" does not hold a light to God's Truth as far as I'm concerned.

MY ENLIGHTMENT

The years of my enlightenment were also the 'dark night of the soul'.

This is not a chapter of my life that I like to remember but I suppose it is one that many people must travel through to find answers to the important questions of life.

I had heard of the 'middle age crises' but never thought it would happen to me. That is what I get for assuming, I guess, because we humans are much more alike than we are different, especially in our carnal state of human nature.

It all started when our sons had left home to marry and make their own way in the world. I was glad for them and wanted to see them 'try their wings,' but had trouble finding mine. I had always said I wanted to enjoy them while they were growing up and be able to let them go when the time came. I think I was able to do that but with a bit more struggle than I had thought. My problem was not in wanting them back home; it was that I did not know what I wanted to do with the rest of my life. I was in my early forties and still healthy and adventuresome.

Tom and I had married very early in our lives. He was almost eighteen and I was barely sixteen. I had gone from being Daddy and Mama's daughter to being Tom's wife and a mother within a short period of time (Fifteen months). When we married, I lacked one year finishing my high school education so I completed that. I was three and a half months pregnant when I graduated and by the time I was twenty-one we had three sons. My life was very busy, to say the least.

Since both Tom and I had been taught responsibility at an early age, we did not see this as a problem. We worked hard, tried to be good parents and did what we had been taught to do – be responsible. We did well financially because neither of us were big spenders and believed in working hard and not wasting things as we had been taught by our parents who lived during the depression. The years spent rearing our boys were good ones. Living on a farm provided opportunities for being busy and we certainly were. The boys helped outside and my job was to take care of the normal household duties. Cleaning, cooking, laundry, shopping, running errands, chauffeuring, etc. kept me hopping. I also did the bookkeeping for the farm business and our small trucking business. When the boys were in high school and later away at college, I took their place helping on the farm. My experiences of these years on the farm, and more, are available in my first book "Gone Are The Days," 'The Family Farm as it was and is.'

After our sons married, one moved away and the other two returned to the family businesses to work with Tom. I found myself with time on my hands, wondering what I should do with the rest of my life.

I had taken a part time job at the local post office as a substitute mail carrier a few years earlier, but it did not require very much of my time – usually only a few days a month.

I also took a few college courses at Western Kentucky University and made an appointment with a counselor to get her advice on what direction I should take. I was considering launching a new career but wasn't sure what I wanted to study. I told her about my affiliation with the postal service and when she found out that it would eventually work into a fulltime job she said, "If I were you I would stay with the postal service since you are already on your way to a good paying position." I guess I was a little disappointed because I assumed since she worked for the college she would encourage me to pursue further education. I understand that a good paying job is the motivation for going to school most of the time but in this instance it was not mine. Maybe I did not make my desires clear and, of course, I did not have to do as she suggested.

However, I did take her advice and did not plan any program for a college degree. I did take some courses now and then to get a taste of it since I had not attended in my earlier years. I took Semantics, Vocabulary, Creative Writing, Spanish and Psychology. I enjoyed the experience but received no real motivation from them. To be totally honest, I was disappointed in the quality of some of the teachers and did not feel inspired or that I learned very much. I guess it did not measure up to my idea of what I thought college was supposed to be.

My part time job became more demanding and eventually I was faced with whether to go full time or not. Since there was no reason why I shouldn't, I bit the bullet. It was the first full-time, away-from-home job I had ever had. I had a lot to learn. (If you want all the details you can read about it in my latest book, "More Than a Job, " 'Making a Difference One Mailbox at a Time').

Since I have always been a reader, thinker and a searcher for truth, and loved the adventure of experiencing new things, I had some adjusting to do. This job cut out most of my time for that and at night I was too tired to read without falling asleep. I was a bit bored with spending so much time driving so I began to check out audio tapes from the library to listen to as I delivered the mail. Fiction has never been my forte so I stuck mostly with non fiction and self-help subjects. I loved M. Scott Peck's books. One of his first, "The Road Less Traveled" whetted my appetite for more. He wasn't a Christian when he wrote it but became a believer later in life. I identified with what he had to say, and wanted to know more. I listened to writers like Deepak Chopra who had a lot to say about 'spiritual' things. Many of the audios the library offered bordered on New Age philosophy. I heard dozens of biographies from Billy Graham to Gloria Steinway. The more I heard, the more I wanted to know. I was still reading my Bible and trying to tie all of it together.

During the process, somewhere along the way I began to feel like I had missed out on being free as a young person, and learning what life was all about. I sought to free myself and capture what I had missed. I enjoyed my work but did not take very much interest in home. I wanted to go places all the time and did, more than at any other time in my life. I did things I had never done before such as fly alone a couple of times to spend a week at my son's house in Kansas and drove to a book fair and stayed overnight by myself. I flew to Paris and rode the rails across Germany to Denmark to visit one of our former exchange students with my middle son and later spent a week in England with a group from the theatre and Georgetown College. These may not seem like huge feats to the modern young woman, but to me they were 'stretching'. I spent a lot of time walking and focused on my physical body more than usual. To sum it up, I was like a typical teenager – pretty wrapped up in myself. When a person is 'wrapped up in themselves' they are not too much benefit to others or the world around them.

Tom had no interest in traveling or adventure, therefore, I neglected him and my affection for him diminished disturbingly. At times I felt I did not love him anymore and if not for the strong convictions I had in the Word of God I'm sure I would have ruined my life and messed up our family horribly by wanting a divorce. Tom got very frustrated with me and if not for divine intervention through the prayers of those that loved me he would have surely given up on our marriage as well.

My heart was far from pure and I knew it. I was filled with guilt. I did not, however, stop going to church and seeking God's help, but became very critical and questioning of it. I now believe the teachings of my parents, the love of my husband who has always been an honest, hard working man, the consistent attendance at church and the Word of God embedded in my mind and heart were like chains holding on to my soul. All of these things together kept me from giving in to what I now recognize as the powers of darkness spoken of in Ephesians 6:10-18. It says. *"Last of all I want to remind you that your strength must come from the Lord's mighty power within you. Put on all of God's armor so that you will be able to stand safe against all strategies and tricks of Satan. For we are not fighting against people made of flesh and blood, but against persons without bodies . . . the evil rulers of the unseen world, those mighty satanic beings and great evil princes of darkness who rule this world; and against huge numbers of wicked spirits in the spirit world."*

"So use every piece of God's armor to resist the enemy whenever he attacks, and when it is all over, you will still be standing up."

"But to do this, you will need the strong belt of truth and the breastplate of God's approval. Wear shoes that are able to speed you on as you preach the Good News of peace with God. In every battle you will need faith as your shield to stop the fiery arrows aimed at you by Satan. And you will need the helmet of salvation and the sword of the Spirit which is the Word of God. Pray all the time.

Ask God for anything in line with the Holy Spirit's wishes. Plead with him, reminding him of your needs, and keep praying earnestly for all Christians everywhere." (TLB - PARAPHASED)

God's armor is surely what protected me when I was too weak spiritually to take care of myself. Scriptures from the Bible are what constantly reminded me of what was right and wrong. In today's society the politically correct way of thinking says there are no absolutes but the Bible teaches differently. If we do not have a plumb line to go by in order to show us when we are off course, we will surely go in every direction that our selfish nature pulls us. It will only end in disaster, like Adam and Eve in the Garden of Eden. Even when we are born again we must guard against the lusts of the flesh with which Satan constantly bombards us. Allowing the Holy Spirit to be our guide is our only hope. How do we do that? By knowing the Word of God and living our lives by its teachings. The two are always in agreement.

The last verse is a very important one also. I will never forget our youngest son coming into my bedroom one morning and telling me of his concern for me and the welfare of our family. Then and there he dropped to his knees and prayed for me. God did not answer his prayer immediately but I'm sure He heard it. I still had some lessons to learn but I will never forget that prayer. It brings tears to my eyes when I think of it and makes me grateful once again for a God that we can depend on when we are weak in spirit.

The following poems are some I wrote during this period of struggle.

Eye of the Soul

When the battles are fierce
And the soul cries in pain,
When there's no clear vision in sight,
The weeping tears of my heart
Stain the colors of the rainbow;
The clouds darken my mind,
Blocking my view
It's then I am reminded of you,
Oh God, my Father!
Your sights are so much higher
So much clearer;
You see the reasons for my pain
And smile in recognition.

The Spirit of Discernment

You make it sound good,
You do all the right things;
You fool most of the people
With your smooth tongue
And sweet sounding words;

Except—what matters most
Is that God is not fooled
No matter the actions
The words or the rules;
He knows the truth
Even when we do not;
Because that is who He is;

The spirit bows low
Makes heavy the heart
The eyes have no shine
The lips cannot smile

Because, they, too
Are part of He who
Is truth from the start:
Why can't we see?
Why don't we know?
That God is not pleased
When we put on a show;

It is only when He
Is allowed to perform
And use our bodies
His name to adorn:
Not try to look good
To others around
Or hide our sins
In words profound.

It is very hard
To allow Him to use
The things that we learn
And often abuse.
For the human mind
Wants glory too.

And people are much
More eager to see
The human beauty
Of you and me;

Because the spirit
Is He who is truth;
And truth is not
Very easy to know!

**Too Many Options**

I long for a simpler time
When life followed need,
No surplus of deciding
Which decision to heed;

The body grew weak
Without any food,
So whatever it took
To find, grow or make
Was what one did
To satisfy the ache;

The sun came up
To brighten the day
So we could see
How to work and play;

When nighttime came
We all gathered in
And snuggled in bed
To rest once again;

In springtime we
Would leap and jump
Along with robins
On field and stump;
The song of bird
Beautiful to hear
Was not drown out
By noises of ear;

When snowflakes fell
Floating to earth
I reached my hand

In merry mirth
And felt the touch
Of dampness soft
On rosy cheek
By winter brought;

Clothes were worn
To keep us warm
No designer names
Of fashion or form;
Knitted and sown
By hands of love
No style compared
To sock or glove;

In the firelight glow
Or by candlelight
Our minds grew big
With images bright
From stories told
In fancy form
By mom or dad
Both night and morn;

No threat of porn
From screen or net,
Not even the books
Were profane yet;
Life was innocent
Play was simple,
A smile was a smile,
A dimple, a dimple;

Mama cooked dinner
Breakfast and lunch

No one complained
About menu or such;
Each one was there,
We knew our place,
And paused to hear
Daddy say 'grace.'
We ate with relish,
We loved every bite;
Our mother's cooking
Was, to us, just right;
Perhaps it helped
We never had snacks
Between our meals
And chores to do
Were more than a few--

Times were hard
Back then they say
But I'm not sure
If it isn't today,
With too many wants
And too few needs
One finds it hard
To truly succeed;

But yesterday is gone,
The present is here
And we must make it
A time to hold dear;
We must choose wisely
How we spend our time
Because so many options
Could blow our mind!

Molde Me, Make Me!

Give me strength to be like precious stones,
Hard, unmovable, yet shiningly beautiful;
Keep my mind at peace, waste it not
On thoughts of hatred, revenge or worry;
Time is Life, and Life is invaluable
Help me use it resourcefully,
Yet with abandon;

Take charge of my motives, desires,
My heart longings;
Make them pure, not self gratifying or envious,
Not only in appearance but all the way through
Because God is not fooled
By self- righteousness in act or thought;
He is only pleased when we give up our stony heart
To be replaced by His heart that is filled with love.

I can truthfully say that Tom and I have a happier marriage today than ever before. I love him much more than I did when we were younger and I believe he does me. I don't believe people have to live a long time to learn this but it is worth the struggle if they do.

The high divorce rate disturbs me intensely. It is one of the things making havoc of our society today. It is a tool that is devastating people's lives, especially the children. Because it is so easy to give up on a marriage, we do not become better people by learning the lessons in life that are necessary for our maturity. When a couple marries, they only see what they like about each other. After the 'honeymoon' period is over, each one reverts back to wanting to do things their way instead of pleasing the other. This is only natural; it is our sinful, selfish nature at work. When God planned marriage between a man and a woman he knew each of us would have to give up a large percentage of 'our way' in order to become 'one' as the Bible says. It isn't easy, but is certainly worth the effort.

Statistics tell us that a much larger percentage of the couples who work through their marriage are happier five years later than the ones who do not. Divorce does not solve all problems; it just creates new ones and most of the time more of them. We have to continue living with one of the people involved, and without a doubt, that person was part of the problem. When we learn and accept that principle we will be going in the right direction to find peace and happiness.

There is a 2008 American Christian drama film by Samuel Goldwyn Films and Sherwood Pictures that deals with this subject. Tom and I saw it and highly recommend it. The name is "Fireproof" and the lead role is Caleb Holt, portrayed by Kirk Cameron. It has action, comedy and is very inspiring.

Stephen Kendrick directed the film and also co-wrote and co-produced it with his brother, Alex Kendrick. The supporting cast is made up of volunteers from Sherwood Baptist Church in Albany, Georgia, where the Kendrick brothers are associate pastors. Other starring characters are Erin Bethea, Ken Bevel, Stephen Dervan and Jason McLeon.

On a budget of $500,000, Fireproof became the highest grossing independent film of 2008 with over $25,000,000 in DVD sales.

Sherwood Baptist Church runs and owns Sherwood Pictures, a film-production company which has produced 'Flywood' and 'Facing the Giants' which are great family films. The company was started by Alex Kendrick with $20,000 in donations.

The success of Sherwood Pictures is an inspiring

example of what Christians can do. It also contradicts the idea that more money can be made with profanity saturated, violent and obscene films.

Not long after the challenge of marriage usually comes another one. Children come into the picture and they are such blessings! They are also frustrating and a lot of work! Our three were not very far apart and the most vivid memory I have of those first years is that I did not get a good night's sleep for five years!

The child rearing years are the best ones if both parents will make it a priority as it should be. One day I asked my ninety year old father which twenty years of his life would he choose to live over to enjoy them again if he was given the opportunity.

He said, "The ones when all the children were home."

I'm afraid our culture convinces young people today that they should have everything immediately- a big house, a new car, fashionable clothes, community status, etc., etc. We have forgotten what 'delayed gratification' is. Both parents usually have to work to accomplish this and they may be able to swing it but when they do they have little time to teach and enjoy the children. Quality time is important but I'm not sure it makes up for quantity. (I know, I know there will always be a huge controversy about working mothers and I'm sure it can work if the circumstances are right. I am certainly not against women working, I just want us to have the happiness and contentment God planned for us.)

When we are willing to make the rearing of our children our priority, we have to give up even more of our selves but I believe that is how God planned it. So many times we want to be the same person we were when we were single and hold on to the things we enjoyed doing with our friends. It doesn't work. We have a higher calling and a much more rewarding one if we will only turn loose of the other. I'm not saying forsake your friends; stay in contact, hold the memories, and make new ones who are in the parenting phase of life. All of this 'giving up of ourselves' sounds unfair but God knows best what we need. Jesus said in Matthew 16:24-26, (NIV) *"If anyone would come after me, he must deny himself and take up his cross and follow me. For whoever wants to save his life will lose it, but whoever loses his life for me will find it. What good is it if a man gains the whole world, yet forfeits his soul? Or what can a man give in exchange for his soul?"* This is a 'hard' saying as Jesus says in another place, but it works.

I believe God planned our life in phases. We pass directly from one to the other, such as from an infant to a toddler, a child, an adolescent, a teenager, young adult, etc. Generally we marry, have children, raise them, and then launch them into adulthood to begin a new cycle. We are then facing middle age, retirement, and old age, if we are exceptionally blessed. Each phase demands acceptance and adjustments. If we embrace each one and let go of the last, it is much less stressful. I have often thought that God knew what He was doing when he planned for children to marry and have their own family before the parents face a natural death. It is so much easier to give them up then. The pain comes when we want to stay where we are and in thinking we know more than God does about how to live our lives. This is especially true in our 'politically correct' world.

Take the subject of abortion, for instance. Why is it right or wrong? Not just because you or I say it is. It is wrong because God says it is. The Bible says life is sacred because we are made in the image of God.

In the first few verses of the ninth chapter of Genesis, Noah and his family have just come out of the ark after the flood and God is blessing them. He had previously given man all of the vegetation for food and now he included all the animals as well. God said to Noah, (verses 4-6) (NIV) *"But you must not eat meat that has its lifeblood still in it. And for your lifeblood I will surely demand an accounting. I will demand an accounting from every animal. And from each man, too, I will demand an accounting for the life of his fellow man. Whoever sheds the blood of man, by man shall his blood be shed; for in the image of God has God made man."*

Let's look at this statement. Why was an animal or a man to be put to death if either killed a person? I believe the answer is because when blood is shed, life is destroyed and life is in the blood. Therefore, any life that has blood in it is sacred to God and is to be protected. In my opinion, this is what should determine when a fetus becomes a human life . . . when there is blood in it.

Animal life is sacred in that the blood must be drained from it before it is eaten. This is still a health practice today, and a good one. The idea comes from the Bible. God also included it in the laws for his people in Deuteronomy 12: 16. *"But you must not eat the blood; pour it out on the ground like water."(NIV)*

In the New Testament, Acts 15: 20, it was included in the three things that the Jewish Council determined was important for the new Gentile Christians to abide by, so it must have been important.

Human life is even more sacred. Life was created by God, in His image, and even though we are very smart, we have not yet figured out how to make it. We can take control of it, manipulate it, kill it, hurt it, dress it up or down and do lots of other things to it but we cannot create it from nothing. We have to have a living cell for creating the egg and sperm to start with. I believe this is another factor determining when life begins. Since God is the one who brought it into existence and placed it on this earth, it stands to reason that He should be the only one who has the wisdom, power and authority to take it away. If you, or I take that decision or power in our hands then we are trying to play God and certainly I am not qualified to do that and I don't think anyone else is either.

As President Obama said, "That is above our pay grade."

This theory is also the one behind embryo cell research, euthanasia, genocide, etc. The shedding of innocent blood is always wrong. War and capital punishments are different in that they are used for self preservation and even then, it is not the way God intended it. He gave us a road map for maturity and the capacity for an abundant life which required neither, but many of us do not choose it and the result is wars and fighting among us. How sad it is that there is peace to be had and we choose not to accept the gift offered. I think, once again, the reason is that we want to do things our way instead of God's way.

This takes us back to the Garden of Eden, doesn't it? I expect it will continue until Jesus returns and takes us to heaven which could possibly be by creating a new earth here. I certainly don't have all of the answers, but I intend to keep believing that His way is best.

STILL LEARNING

It has been almost six years since I retired from the Postal Service and I have become a student again. In fact, I suppose I have never stopped being one and hopefully never will as long as there is life in my bones. Learning, whatever the avenue, is what makes life exciting for me.

While I was driving around delivering mail I could think of all kinds of things I would like to do if only I had the time. I figured God must have something important for me to do and I was eager to get at it. After questioning this idea and vehemently barraging the throne of God with my prayers for answers about what His plan for me was, the light finally began to shine through.

I had more lessons to learn about what is important to God and that our ways are not His ways.(Isaiah 55:8&9)

I was of the opinion that one must be engaged in some important activity in order to achieve productivity.

Wrong!

I also had the tendency to think that in order to be a student and further your education one has to enroll in an institute of higher learning.

Wrong again!

This is not to say that one will not learn by doing this but it will only be what everyone else that takes the course learns with the exception of a few who have that blessed thing called 'initiative'. I tend to like individual information from a source I know I can depend on to be authentic. To achieve this, God has to get us still and willing to listen before we can hear Him clearly.

I tried a few projects that I thought might be something that could make a positive contribution to society and every time an uncalculated circumstance interfered. I had no other recourse but to believe that these interferences were in His plan since I was truly seeking His will for me. Since I have always been a 'take charge' person, it took quite a few lessons for me to learn to wait on God.

As my eyes are beginning to be opened I see things I have never observed before. I used to see life as how much a person can squeeze out of it by staying busy doing all you can, learning all you can, and enjoying it all you can while helping everyone you can in the process. Now I see it as not having to rush from one thing in order to get to the next, but living in the present so that I will not miss anything that God has for me in the current situation. I have learned if I reduce my spending I don't have to spend my precious hours working and can use them in whatever opportunity that comes my way. An example of this is helping my husband and sometimes our grandson go to the woods and cut up fallen trees to use for burning in our fireplace this past winter. Rewards are mine in many different ways. I really enjoy the feeling of doing something physically to provide necessities for my well being; I love the warmth and coziness that comes from sitting in front of the open fire in the evenings; it is good exercise for me; it cleans up the fields making a nicer landscape on the farm; it saves on our electric bill each month and is a good environmental activity. Another benefit is having the opportunity to spend time with our grandson and paying him, instead of the utility company, so he will have the opportunity to learn how to manage his money as well as a power saw. An added bonus is that he gets to experience manual labor which I believe is good for all of us now and then.

I think it may also be nostalgic for me because it brings

back memories of working in the woodpile with my brother while growing up. We sawed the wood with a six-foot-long crosscut saw that had a handle on each end, and split some of it up for using in the wood-burning cooking stove that our mother cooked on in the kitchen. The rest of it was used for our fireplace or warm morning heater in the living room. Each evening it was our job to carry enough inside to be used until the next evening. Believe it or not, I had a pretty bad swing on me when splitting those sawed pieces that were too big for the stoves.

See what I mean by my eyes and mind being opened to new ways of thinking. For many years I believed in "seizing the day", now I believe in 'seizing every moment.' That insight may come partly because of age but in order to relish life completely, I am convinced that I need to seek to know God better in every way so that I will not miss the best things in life that He has promised to give me. More and more I notice people attempting to enjoy life, have fun and get the most out of it while only fooling themselves by making the same mistakes I did.

As I mentioned before, in the scriptures Jesus said the most important thing for a person to do is love the God with all their heart, mind and soul, and love their neighbor as themselves. That is quite a challenge and one that I take seriously. It is amazing how that it works in sequence. When I contemplate the extent of what God has done for me; from the very breath I breathe physically to his dying for me so that I can have true life in His spirit, my heart cannot help but overflow with love for him. That love, in turn, fills my heart with love for my family and others . . . even my enemies. Nothing is more important than loving our families and those around us, while passing on to them the faith that will sustain them in the years to come and help them to do the same for their children and grandchildren. To overlook mistakes they make (I can recognize many of them because I made the same ones when I was their age) and most of all, trust God to give them wisdom and understanding that I want them to have but can in no way give to them. I can see that as a parent I made many mistakes because I was not mature enough to realize what a responsible and important position we had been given. I can see that I was more interested in my dreams being fulfilled than in preparing our children for life. I have asked for forgiveness and pray regularly that God will make up in their lives what we failed to give them so that they will not make the same mistakes we did. I believe He will.

My five siblings and I take turns staying in my mother's home and taking care of her, usually in twenty-four-hour intervals. I see this as an opportunity not as an interruption in my life. It is like having a Sabbath on whatever day is my turn. We have certain tasks to do but there is much time for reflection, meditation and solo activities that give us a chance to know ourselves better and spend time in getting to know our creator as well. It also creates a stronger bond with my siblings who I would not see nearly as often if we were not involved in our mother's care. Often times we only know our parents and siblings as we did growing up. To get to know them as the adults they have become since that time is a new experience. It has also proven to be good 'alone' time for our spouses, maybe not coveted time always, but good for personal growth.

Another plus is that many people do not slow down their activities until bad health demands it. This has given us a chance to slow down and 'smell the roses' while we are still healthy enough to enjoy all of them.

Revelations keep coming and I keep being astonished at how much there is to learn. Old age and a deteriorating body are not positive things but wisdom that comes with age and experience sure help to make it more enjoyable.

The years since I retired have been kind of like a sabbatical, giving me time to reassess things, rethink what is most important to me and regroup. Only God knows when and if I am ready to take on a new challenge. I am trying to trust Him completely in the process. I want to get it right this time, by most standards I don't have as much time and energy left as I once did.

On the other hand, my mother almost made it to her one hundredth birthday.

The Bible *reveals the mind of God, the state of man, the way of salvation, the doom of sinners, and the happiness of believers. Its doctrines are holy, its precepts binding, its histories are true, its decisions are immutable. Read it to be wise, believe it to be safe, and practice it to be holy. It contains light to direct you, food to support you, and comfort to cheer you. It is the traveler's map, the pilgrim's staff, the pilot's compass, the soldier's sword and the Christian's charter. Here, Heaven is opened and the gates of hell disclosed. Christ is its grand subject, our good is its design, the glory of God its end. It should fill your memory, rule your heart, and guide the feet. Read it slowly, frequently, and prayerfully. It is given in life, will be opened in the judgement, and will be remembered forever. It involves the highest responsibility, will reward the greatest labor, and will condemn all those who trifle with its sacred contents. Owned, it is riches; studied, it is wisdom; trusted, it is salvation; loved, it is character; and obeyed, it is power.*

~ Author Unknown